"*God's Love*

Available in book stores & at
www.Godslovein3-dimensions.com
For Direct Book Purchasing
or
Speaking Engagements
Contact Jim McGrew at 211 S. Wood,
Odin, IL 62870 • Ph. (618) 775-8238

God's Love In 3-Dimensions

Jim McGrew

Bloomington, IN  Milton Keynes, UK

AuthorHouse™
1663 Liberty Drive, Suite 200
Bloomington, IN 47403
www.authorhouse.com
Phone: 1-800-839-8640

AuthorHouse™ *UK Ltd.*
500 Avebury Boulevard
Central Milton Keynes, MK9 2BE
www.authorhouse.co.uk
Phone: 08001974150

© *2007 Jim McGrew. All rights reserved.*

No part of this book may be reproduced, stored in a retrieval system, or transmitted by any means without the written permission of the author.

First published by AuthorHouse 3/13/2007

ISBN: 978-1-4259-8170-9 (sc)
ISBN: 978-1-4259-8169-3 (hc)

Cover Designed by Jim Wiedman

Printed in the United States of America
Bloomington, Indiana

This book is printed on acid-free paper.

Special Acknowledgments and Thanks to: Tom Smith, Lois Albert, my wife Sandra and our daughter Cindy for their editing. And I give thanks to Michelle Hassebrock, and our son Brent for their much needed help on the computer. They each have been a blessing to me.

Above all I give thanks and praise, to my Heavenly Father, and my Lord and Savior, who gave me something glorious to write about. Only by their Holy Word and the divine intervention of the Holy Spirit was the writing of "God's Love in 3- Dimensions" accomplished.

Table of Contents

INTRODUCTION	X
CHAPTER ONE: "GOD'S LOVE FOR US"	1
The Supremacy of Christ our Creator	2
The clock that lost its function.	4
Our Heartbreaking Tragedy!	10
What is Our Function as Members of Christ Body, The Church?	20
The three wills of God.	24
Gods Love for us, surrounds us, and fills us.	26
Jesus is the Way to God's love and freedom.	28
Why God shed the blood of His One and Only Begotten Son!	30
The Greatest News the World has ever Received!	33
God's Blood Covenants!	34
Jesus sacrificed His Life Blood for all the worlds!	36
What Must We Do to Complete God's Blood Covenant of Love?	38
Jesus comes to us, and we come to Jesus by the way of the cross!	39
The prophecy of God's great sacrifice and love for us!	41
Living in the 3-Dimensions of God's Gift of Love!	46
Viewing "God's Love for us!"	49
Viewing the Road to Calvary!	50
The Price Jesus Paid for us at Mount Calvary!	50
"God's Love for US" was measured at Calvary!	52
Questionnaire	55
CHAPTER TWO: "OUR LOVE FOR GOD"	61
What is the true purpose of life?	61
God shows us the way to express "our love for God," through Jesus!	63
"Our love for God" is to walk the walk of Jesus!	67

Jesus teaches us to Pray!	69
"Our love for God" intertwines within our relationships with others.	72
"True Love Relationships"	75
Three important truths that must exist in a "True love relationship."	76
#-1---Love must be voluntary!	76
#-2—Love must be reciprocal!	78
#-3—Love Must be Based on Trust!	81
Through sacrifice we express "our love for God."	83
"Our love for God" Is Following God's Commandments!	86
The cause of divisions in the Church.	93
The importance of knowing and following the commandments of Jesus.	95
"Our love for God" is expressed in proper and pleasing giving.	97
True and proper worship.	101
"Our Love for God" is being an ambassador for Christ!	102
Claude the Caterpillar and Barney the Butterfly	103
"Our love for God" must far exceed all others, and all things, in our lives!	105
Jesus Requirements, and Reinstatement, of a Fallen Disciple!	112
Questionnaire	115
CHAPTER THREE: "LOVE FOR ONE ANOTHER"	**121**
The Importance of Knowing and Sharing God's Love.	124
Clothing ourselves daily in Christ!	126
Following the Golden Rule!	129
Making Jesus Lord of Our lives is the Doorway to "love for one another."	134
"Love for one another," is sharing one another's burdens.	141
The New Commandment of Jesus brings fulfillment to our lives, and completes God's love in us.	148
Following Jesus is Becoming Like Jesus!	149
Learning to "Love one another" as Jesus Loved us.	153
"love is patient."	154

"Love is Kind."	158
"Love keeps no record of wrongs."	163
With the cross of Jesus ever before us, our life resides in God's love!	166
Unveiling God's Love!	167
Our Goal and Destiny	168
Questionnaire	172
REFERENCE PAGE	177

INTRODUCTION

Could there be anything more exciting and blessed assurance in our life than knowing that the creator of the universe loves us? That is what this book "God's love in 3-dimensions" is about, God's love for us, and His designed purpose for our lives; Reflecting back over more than forty years of service in the Body of Christ; I have found the most important things to be taught and expressed, to bring love and unity, and success to the life of the Church, and to our personal lives are, "God's love for us," "Our love for God," and "Our love for one another." For the success and the life of the Church, and for our personal lives, God's love must prevail. "God's Love in 3-dimensions" reiterates the plea of the writings of our Lord's Apostles, and the prayer of our Lord, for love and unity.

The apostles of our Lord pleaded for us throughout the scriptures to have love and unity through the Spirit of God's love. Jesus our Lord prayed for God's unity and love for His followers; **"that all of them may be one, Father, just as you are in Me and I am in You." "I have made You known to them, and will continue to make You known in order that the <u>love</u> You have for Me may be in them and that I Myself may be in them."**(John 17:21&26). What great accomplishments and success await us when we walk in unity with our Lord and Heavenly Father. The greatness of God's love, joy and peace fills our hearts, souls and minds, providing divine direction and assurance as we walk in our Lord's Spirit of love. And what great accomplishments have been made by the body of Christ when our Lord's love and unity prevail among His body members, when working together in the directives and spirit of their Lord.

What creates and produces unity with the Heavenly Father, within us, and within the body of Christ? God's love! What motivated God's plan of salvation for mankind? God's love! What power innovated and sustained our Lord, and Savior, in carrying out God's plan of salvation? God's love! What would be the greatest and most significant news a person could receive? God loves you! What is the greatest and most significant news one could ever share with another? God loves you! What brings unity and peace within our individual selves, and the Lord's Church? The knowledge, the receiving, and the expression of God's love!

This book is written through the spiritual desire to glorify and praise the Triune God Head, for their love.

CHAPTER ONE:
"God's Love for Us"

"God's love for us" has placed a great value on our lives and has made each one of us unique and special. Let me give you what I believe to be a universal truth "Order and complexity never arise spontaneously; they are always generated by a prior cause programmed to produce such order." You are not a happening! You are a unique child of your Heavenly Father, created for a special purpose and destiny.

Do you realize that in all the worlds, and in all the billions of people, no one is quite like you? Your Creator has designed and carved in intricate detail a special print upon the fingers and thumbs of your hands, when you raise up holy hands to your Heavenly Father; He will know you as His child, by His prints upon your hands. And of all the voices in the world, no voice is quite like yours. If you cry out Abba Father, the Heavenly Father hears and knows your voice, as His unique and special child.

Jesus said: **"See that you do not look down on one of these little ones. For I tell you that their angels in heaven always see the face of my Father in heaven."** (Matthew 18:10) Our Heavenly Father's love for us has assigned each of his children a Guardian Angel. Therefore, let us be aware and on guard of how we treat the objects of God's love, for God hates haughty eyes. (Prov. 6:17.) Eyes which look down on another are projected from a heart without love. Use care and love in the treatment of the

1

children of God, for the insults that fall on the children of God, falls on their Heavenly Father.

Why are you so special to your Heavenly Father? Because you have been created in the very image of the triune God head for a divine purpose and destiny. You are the object of God's love. He is the lover of your soul. Our Heavenly Father has sent unto us His one and only begotten Son, the image of the invisible God, that we through Jesus might reach the destiny, the purpose, and blessings for which we were created. In order to look further into God's love for us, let us look intently into God's Holy word, one of His love letters written to us.

The Supremacy of Christ our Creator

The Holy Scripture's says this about Jesus, **"He is the image of the invisible God, the firstborn over all creation. For by Him all things were created: things in heaven and earth, visible and invisible, whether thrones or powers or rulers or authorities; all things were created by Him and for Him. He is before all things, and in Him all things hold together. And He is the head of the body, the church; He is the beginning and the firstborn from among the dead, so that in everything He might have the supremacy. For God was pleased to have all fulness dwell in Him, and through Him to reconcile to Himself all things, whether things on earth or things in heaven, by making peace through His blood, shed on the cross."** (Colossians 1:15-20.)

- God is an Omnipotent, Sovereign, Transcendent Spirit. God has unlimited power and authority. God is the creator and supreme ruler of the universe. God is all knowing, and able to be at all places at all times as he chooses. God is a supreme eternal being of dimensions that reaches beyond our comprehension and yet God leaves us many footprints of His existence, and of His love for us.

But the most significant proven historical fact God gave us of His existence, and His love for us, was Jesus. The Word and Spirit of God became flesh and walked amongst us. Within us is the need to touch and be touched, to hold and be held. Our Heavenly Father reached out to us through Jesus. Jesus became the physical image of the living God that we might see, and touch, and behold God. Through Jesus, God has reached out and touched our lives with the needs of our lives. Through Jesus, God opened up His heart and soul to us, pouring out His love upon us. Seeing and knowing Jesus, is seeing and knowing our omnipotent, sovereign, transcendent God. In Jesus, God said: this is who I am; in Christ God exposed to us His heart of love and grace for each of us.

In these short scriptures of God's Holy word we are given many facets of the identity of Jesus:

- We find that Jesus is God.
- We find that by Jesus all things were created, things in heaven and on earth.
- We find that we were created by Jesus and for Jesus.
- We find that in Jesus all things hold together.
- We find that Jesus is the head of the body, the Church.
- We find that it pleased God, to have all of the fulness of His Spirit dwell in Jesus. **"For in Christ all the fullness of the Deity lives in bodily form."** (Colossians 2:9)

- We find that all things reconciled to the Heavenly Father must come through Jesus. Jesus said, **"I am the way and the truth and the life. No one comes to the Father except through me."** (John 14:6)

- We find that our peace comes by the way of the cross through the shed blood of Gods perfect Lamb, our Lord and Savior.

In Jesus we discover our own identity we understand where we came from and to whom we belong. Not only were all things created through Jesus, He is also able to maintain all things, which includes you and me when we choose as free will beings, to place our lives in the Hands of our Maker. The scripture in verse seventeen should be carried in the memory of the mind and heart of every Christian; "in Jesus all things hold together." Every Christian should carry this good news to everyone they meet "In Jesus all things hold together." In order to further explain the importance of Jesus and how He causes life to function properly, and that in Him all things hold together, I would like to relate a story from personal experience. The story concerns my mantel clock:

THE CLOCK THAT LOST ITS FUNCTION.

After being transferred to Houston, Texas, I discovered that my mantel clock no longer worked. My wife Sandra had purchased the clock at the Lincoln Trail Antique store for my birthday. Though I am not a clock maker, and even though I had never repaired a clock, it took me only a short time to figure out how to repair my clock. I quickly decided that all the clock needed was a good cleaning of its working mechanisms. By quick inspection, I could see right away how I could clean the entire working mechanisms of my clock. Proud of my discovery, I carried the clock into the

Chapter One: "God's Love For Us"

kitchen where my lovely wife was, so that I might explain to her how I was going to repair our clock. I very simply told her how the clock's working mechanisms slid onto a shaft, and all I needed to do, was to carefully remove the little nut at the end of the shaft, then slide the entire clock mechanism off the shaft. I would then dip the clock's mechanisms into some cleaning fluid, let it dry out, and put it back in place. I told her I was sure the clock would then run just fine after this simple repair.

Now, after fully explaining to her what I was going to do, guess what her response was, my fellow men? She said: "I wouldn't do that if I were you!" I stood astonished and upset with her. For had I not just fully explained to her how I knew what I was doing and she responds with; "I wouldn't do that if I were you!" She had just questioned my intellect. She was saying that I did not know what I was doing! Well, she might just as well have said, "sic um" to a bull dog. What audacity! Now instead of returning to my work bench, I would now have to remove the clock's mechanisms right in front of her. She would have to be shown that I knew what I was doing! Slowly, right in her face, I began to unscrew the little nut that would free the clock's mechanism and allow me to prove my point. As I was turning the little brass nut on the last turn, something suddenly occurred, the likes of which I have never seen before. A brass plate flew in front of me! And following the brass plate was a mass of little gears, springs, and things flying through the air and falling onto the kitchen floor. I stood for a moment in shock! I then got a broom and dust pan and began to sweep up all my clocks' parts, and though I swept in total silence I felt I could hear the words; "I told you so." I proceeded to put all my clocks, gears, springs, and things of which I had never seen before into a little brown paper bag. Why I did that I really don't know, for if I could shake that sack for the next million years, all those parts would not fall back together, and that would be the extent of my ability. There was no one now who could put my clock back together. I had destroyed it. Maybe I swept up my clock parts and placed them in the little brown paper sack so I would not have to look at my wife's face that must have had a little smirk that was saying: "I told you so." My poor clock looked like a clock but it would never function as a clock again, for it had fallen into the wrong hands. Sandra was kind enough to never mention to me the stupid thing I did to my clock, though I am relatively sure that she loved telling the story to others. For one day my son's girl friend, Kelly, came to me and said that her dad could put my clock back together. Our son, Greg, and Kelly were both 19 yrs of age and had met at college.

    I explained to Kelly what had happened and that there was no one who could possibly put my clock back together. She replied: "Give me your clock and I will take it to my father and he will put it back together." At that point I became somewhat aggravated, evidently she had not understood what I had said. In order to emphasize what I had said, I told her: "Kelly, see this little brown bag. This little brown sack is full of all sorts of little gears, springs, and things never seen before." I swept up the pieces after this nut standing in front of you removed the little brass nut that allowed the insides of my clock to fly out and onto the kitchen floor. Now no one can put this mess back together, nor would I ask anyone to try such a task, for if I was to shake this bag for the next million years, these little pieces would never fall back into their proper place." (Which I had by now, humbly come to realize, shaking a bag was the extent of my ability in clock repair.) To this Kelly replied: "Give me your clock and the parts and my father will put it back together." I thought what a persistent young lady, and somewhat aggravated with her unwillingness to give in, I gave in and said: "Ok you may take the clock," thinking to myself her father will soon send her back with that clock and its bag of mixed up parts.

    A few weeks had passed by when one night Kelly invited us over to meet her parents, Bob and Joyce Sholten. Her parents were very nice people. Bob worked for the airlines and our son Greg worked part time for the airlines. Joyce worked for the school system. As the evening progressed, Kelly's father invited me into a side room to show me something. As I entered the room, I saw the walls lined with clocks. Some of the clocks were beautiful grandfather clocks, and all the clocks were ticking and keeping perfect time. Looking around the room I saw my clock sitting on a shelf among all the clocks, and it was ticking and keeping time with all the rest of the clocks! You see Kelly's father was also a clock maker. Before we left that night, Bob gave me my clock and some final instructions on how to care for my clock. Now, nineteen years later, my clock is still ticking and keeping perfect time. Precious memories often flood my mind when I wind my clock.

Like the clock, our lives too can be strewn apart when placed in the wrong hands. And unless some persistent soul leads you to your Maker, your life will never run right. Jesus, the Maker of our souls, can make our life like a Timex-we can "take a licking and keep on ticking." A prophecy of Jesus says: "A bruised reed He will not break, and a smoldering wick He will not snuff out." (Isaiah 42:3). What seems useless and almost spent to the world, God's love for us through His servant our Lord, will restore us and make us whole and useful again. Jesus our Lord told us that in this world we will have many trials and tribulations. But, take heart, I have overcome the world! (John 16:33) The one who made you will see you through this world and keep you right on ticking, and keeping time to the divine purpose for which your Lord created you. When we lose our Lord's divine designed purpose in life, our lives become dysfunctional. Tragedy and death await those who choose to take the side road of life, which leads us away from the life of Christ. We can close the door of our heart, and the door of the Church that closes out Christ, and write Ichabod across them. For without Christ, the head of our lives and the head of the Church, we are but a breathless body. Therefore, we need to make Jesus the supreme head of our personal lives and the body of the Church. For, "in Jesus all things hold together." <u>How do we make Jesus supreme in our lives and the life of the Church?</u>

<u>First</u>, we need to always remember we are His, and the Church is His. Christ gave birth to His Church when the Apostle Peter spoke the gospel message of Jesus for the first time on the first day of the week, through the enabling power of the Baptism of the Holy Spirit. And that is why Sunday is called the "Lord's Day." We ourselves were created by Jesus, and for Jesus. When we place our faith in our creator as Lord and Savior of our lives, we then, through the cleansing of the word and blood of Jesus, become children of the Heavenly King and royal heirs of the riches of His Spirit. All this should compel us to love and serve Jesus as Lord of our lives, making Him supreme in our lives and the life of His Church.

<u>Secondly</u>, we must make Jesus supreme in our lives by acknowledging him as Lord and Director of our lives. How do we do that? We do it by speaking with Jesus as our Lord and friend in all our plans, asking for His divine intervention and divine guidance in our daily walk. Also we do it by listening to, and following daily the directives of our Lord, through his written word and His Spirit, He places in our hearts. We accomplish this by getting into our Lord's word and placing it on the front burner of our hearts and minds. The early Church set forth the example of how to make Jesus supreme in our lives, and the life of His church. We read in Acts 2:42: **"They devoted themselves to the Apostles' teaching."** When we get into the word of the Lord, then the Spirit of the Lord gets into our lives and the life of the Church. The early Church devoted their selves **"to the fellowship." "And let us consider how we may spur one another on toward love and good deeds. Let us not give up meeting together, as some are in the habit of doing, but let us encourage one another— and all the more as you see the Day approaching."** (Hebrew's 10:24-25.) Our lives need the fellowship of fellow believers. They devoted themselves **"to the breaking of bread."** The breaking of bread in this scripture refers to the Lord's supper. **"The Lord**

Chapter One: "God's Love For Us"

Jesus, on the night He was betrayed, took bread, and when He had given thanks, He broke it and said, "This is my body, which is for you; do this in remembrance of me." In the same way, after supper He took the cup, saying, "This cup is the new covenant in my blood; do this whenever you drink it, in remembrance of me." (1 Corinthians' 11:23-25.) They devoted themselves **"to prayer."** Christians should never begin a day, or make a decision without consulting their Lord in prayer. **"Trust in the Lord with all your heart and lean not on your own understanding; in all your ways acknowledge Him, and He will make your paths straight."** (Proverbs 3:5&6.) In order to make Jesus supreme in our lives and the life of His Church, we need to <u>devote ourselves</u> to the teaching of God's word, to the fellowship, to the breaking of bread, and to prayer.

<u>Thirdly</u>–in making Jesus supreme in our lives and the life of the Church body, we must allow Christ to reign in us and rule through us. To help us in doing this, we must place this truth in our mind and apply it in our lives; true Christianity is more than a religion, to be a true disciple of our Lord we must have a personal relationship with Jesus our Lord and Savior, and even more than that a true discipleship is becoming like Jesus, "walking as our Lord walked." And when we walk with the Lord, the Lord creates good works through us. When we give Jesus supremacy in our lives and the life of His Church, Jesus will change and cleanse our hearts and minds. He does this through the power of His word, and by filling us with His Spirit of love, making us vessels of His love, for good works. This is the empowering work of "God's love for us." Living in the word and the spirit of our Lord, places our lives in the hands of our maker, and keeps us from becoming dysfunctional like the clock that fell into the wrong hands.

Like clocks, People need their maker. But unlike clocks when people become dysfunctional, the effect carries over into the hearts, minds, and souls of those near them. They can feel the depths of pain and despair to the point of near death. And we can see and feel the pain and despair of loved ones near us. Like many others, our family has experienced the depths of pain and despair. I have clung to my faith in God, like one clinging to the side of a mountain. For, in the time of our despair and grief I knew that only God could see us through the mountain of despair we faced. In the beginning I would at times be angry at God, and would question why God would allow such devastation to occur. And I guess some question of why will remain with me until I see my Lord face to face, and He lifts the veil of wonder from my heart. I know that God and His Love for us will see us through, whatever problems we face, if we place our faith in Him. Maybe God will enable our mind and heart with ideas and compassion to where we can overcome the problem that we face. Maybe God will send someone into our life to help us overcome the problem that we face. And then again maybe the problem we are facing is a mountain that is too high to overcome. It is then when God will give us the strength and comfort to live with it. My family has experienced the depths of pain, of suffering, and the despair of a broken heart. And I have experienced the healing Spirit of God's Love, where he enabled me to live with the life changing tragedy in our life.

Our Heartbreaking Tragedy!

I mentioned Greg in the clock story. We lost Greg shortly thereafter in a car accident. He was going to pick up Kelly when his car hydroplaned into an oncoming car. I have just returned to the key board and I would like to tell you that everything is all right! But the truth is, I just returned from being on my knees weeping for my beloved son, and asking God to help us. It has been nineteen years ago that we were a family of five which included my wife Sandra, our daughter Cindy who had graduated from Southern Illinois University, our son Greg who graduated

Chapter One: "God's Love For Us"

from Odin High School and was attending a junior college and working part time at the Houston airport and our youngest son Brent, who was twelve years old. We had lived all our lives in a small community and we had no desire to move to a large city. I was employed by Texaco pipeline. Inc. The refinery had closed and that meant many would lose their jobs. I remember driving home from work one evening and thinking about being transferred, and for some reason California came into my mind, and then suddenly my chest turned ice cold; it was a feeling like I had never felt before. But I would feel this feeling one more time. Later I was offered a transfer to Houston, Texas. My wife Sandra and I prayed about the transfer one evening in our bedroom. I asked the Lord for divine guidance and said to Him that we had decided not to take the transfer and that we would put our faith in Him. A week later one of the supervisors asks me if they had offered me any severance pay. I replied no, for I had not quit my job, but I went home and told my wife what had been said. After speaking with my wife about the matter, I decided to go in and speak with the district manager. He told me he felt he would have the pipeline sold by May. I began searching for another job in the area but receiving nothing, we became scared of not having income to raise our family and I decided to take the transfer. The pipeline did not sell and had I refused the transfer I would not have lost my job. Had I kept faith in God, and had I listened to the coldness I had felt in my chest, I would not have taken the transfer. I would receive that coldness, like ice across my chest one more time.

When Greg was small, I never wanted to see him fall, never to be hurt, I always wanted to protect him. I remember watching him when he was small, watching cartoons and he would cry for Bambi. He was always so tenderhearted. I baptized Greg into Christ when he was a small boy. In many ways spiritually I felt he had outgrown me. Greg loved life like no one I had ever known; he seemed to enjoy and get the most out the smallest things in life. He was always so appreciative of life, and the things we did for him. I can never remember Greg to ever criticize people or be critical of the things you did. I can remember more than once of people complaining about teenagers. My response was always the same, "I have a teenager who is always a blessing to me." He never wanted to disappoint us. I remember after Greg's death a friend of mine said to me that Greg was a friend to his son. He told me that not everyone was, for he was a little slower than some and not always accepted. I thanked him for telling me that, I knew that would be true of Greg. I loved Greg's spirit, we were bonded spiritually, and will be throughout all eternity. Greg was my catcher on a pony league team that I managed, and our friend Claude Howell was our left-hand pitcher. Claude is now senior Minister at Evergreen Christian Church. We will always wonder until the Lord calls us home how much more blessed our lives would have been had Greg not left us. We were at a church social one day when an elderly lady walked up behind us and said, "That is the most handsome young man I have ever seen." I replied to her, "Ma'am, he can't help that, the Lord made him that way." Greg inherited the beauty of his mother and her hair.

Greg's hair was dark and wavy and laid perfectly in place. He was easy to look at, but more than that he was easy to love. The measure of our loss and grief is measured by our relationship, and we had a deep love relationship. I remember the minster friend of ours saying at the funeral that we would have to pick up the pieces and put them back together. I can only remember thinking how can we do that, for a piece of our family and life is missing. A piece of our heart was removed and will not be replaced until we meet Greg again in the Heavenly Kingdom of our Lord.

Sandra and I, and our son Brent returned to our home in Texas after the funeral. When we arrived about 10:00 P.M. the little boy who lived next door, whose name was P J, came out to greet us, when we drove in the drive way. He said; "How are you all doing?" We said, "Not so good PJ." Then we walked alone into a

Chapter One: "God's Love For Us"

dark house to where the imprint of our son had been lying. I only remember thinking if I don't get back outside I'm going to die. I can't remember what happened the rest of the night or many days after we arrived. I can only say today, if I ever knew of anyone driving to what lay ahead of us, I would ask them to move over, for I'm going with you, it's too much to bear alone.

A few nights later after we had arrived back, we drove into our drive way, Sandra was driving and I was riding on the passenger side. Suddenly a car pulled in the driveway on Sandra's side. I looked over at the car. The car had a radiant shine like a jewel. It was Greg's car! And I said, "That's Greg!" I jumped out of the car and rushed around to the front of the cars and there in front of the cars Greg and I met each other. I began to speak to him, but he held his finger up to his mouth to quiet me. Then we held out our arms and we hugged, but as I was hugging him a cold feeling came across my chest. And then I sat up, awakened in our bed, and my chest felt like ice. I don't know if it was a dream or vision I had experienced; I just know I have never experienced anything so real and vivid. And nineteen years later it is still that vivid and real. To me he was saying, "I'm ok!" Many times I have prayed that God would give my wife and children a vision of Greg so they would know he is ok so they could be ok. But as far as I know, they have never received a vision. Why? I don't know.

After our great tragedy I went through a period of numbness and knowing I could die. I know now a person can die of a broken heart. There was a part of me that wanted to die and be with Greg. But another was pulling me to stay and not hurt or forsake the remainder of my family. I was torn between two worlds. I made a decision that I had a responsibility to the people I loved in this world. I went back to work trying to place one foot in front of the other. I can only remember short clips of what occurred the next few months. I remember walking beside our district manger Gerald Schultz one day after returning to work. Gerald placed his hand on my shoulder and I broke down. I would withhold my emotions after that, pushing past memories out of my mind. I want to take time here to say thanks to Gerald for helping me in getting my family back to our home in Illinois. I vividly remember a painful experience while working alone at a pump station one night. Past memories began to flash through my mind. I tried to shut them out, but they were uncontrollable, like short flashes of lightning they continued flashing pictures and memories of the past through my mind. Today I cherish those memories I tried to forget, they are not painful as they were then. Another memory clip I have of those first few months is one while being alone again while at work in the field. I became violently angry at God for allowing Greg to die. Later my thoughts would turn to knowing that if I lost my faith, and the presence of God, I would lose everything. I prayed fervently with a broken heart and broken home for healing. Beyond the time I spent with Sandra and Brent, and at work, I spent time taking a correspondence course on the Old Testament from Johnson Bible College. I also spoke at a newly formed Church called New Hope until we were transferred. One of my regrets and hurt in leaving to return to Illinois was leaving behind the people of that Church body.

We returned back to our home in Illinois where my prayers continued for a closer presence of God. And at times I would write to our son Greg. I have never shared the writings with anyone but my wife. One of the prayers that I prayed I will share with you. It was a prayer I prayed so many times that I began to sing it to the Lord while driving alone. This is the prayer, the plea, the song, that I prayed;

CHAPTER ONE: "GOD'S LOVE FOR US"

"In His Hand"

Lift me up Lord, lift me up Lord,
By the strength of your Hand.

Hold me tightly, hold me tightly,
don't let me fall away,
Lift me higher and higher
by the power of thy Hand.

That I might feel your presence
dwelling in me.

Let me drink Lord, let me drink Lord,
from the cup of your Hand.

Of your Spirit and Kindness
let it flow through me.

Let me serve you, let me serve you,
from the cup of your Hand.

Lift me higher in your service,
by the guiding of your Hand.

In His Hand

Chapter One: "God's Love For Us"

I will also share with you something I have written of my son, and to my son. Looking back into my old note book, I now see an attitude and faith placed in these words, which I believe helped sustain me, as the Lord restored my soul, and the will to live. I hope they may help you in some way.

"Two Worlds Apart"

We are two worlds apart, and it breaks my heart.
Being here without you tears my world apart.
We are two worlds apart, but our love won't part.
We are bonded and sealed together forever.

We are two worlds apart, while I sojourn here
you have arrived at the destiny for which my
Heart yearns.

We are two worlds apart, but bonded and sealed
Together forever, by His Love we shared
while we journeyed here.

Chapter One: "God's Love For Us"

"In memory of my beloved son"

Relationships cannot be measured in years of time gone by;
Lasting relationships are measured by the pouring out of God's Love
Into our hearts, and from one heart to another, and the love
   we received and shared will bond our Spirits forever.

The calender on the wall says time has gone by
   and I've missed you so much. But, the cross
   on Calvary says the future is ours.

Time can't touch God, or take His Love away;
   the love He gave us will be ours forever.

And I know it's true, for the love we shared remains and will forever.

There is only one gift. We can leave behind–thank
   you Greg for sharing with me God's great gift.

Hey Greg we'll

be seeing you.
Love Dad.

What is Our Function as Members of Christ Body, The Church?

I remember our minister back in Texas invited us over to his home and showed us a Laurel and Hardy movie. I know he was trying to help, but it wasn't the help we needed. We were so all alone neither the company I worked for, nor the church that we attended, nor the school Brent attended, ever offered any counseling that I see now we needed so desperately. Today I see ministers and Church bodies so involved in the building of their church, by showing a positive mode of how happy they are, that one would be afraid of entering in under any other response to their greeting, than I am great, for fear of not being accepted. I've seen worship services where song leaders wanted to see everyone singing with a smile on their face. I've seen a time when my heart was so broken I would break down and cry when I tried to sing. I tried to sing because I thought that it was expected of me by the Church. But do you know what? God never expected that of me. We find written in Gods Holy Word **"Is anyone among you suffering? Then he must pray. Is anyone cheerful? He is to sing praises."**(James 5:23) We set a large portion of our service for the cheerful to sing praises. Are we providing a time in our ministry and service for the suffering? I know Jesus did; He left the ninety-nine to tend to one.

If the church is truly the Body of Christ, then we as members of Christ's Body must respond as Christ's Body did. Jesus always walked in the love and the will of the Heavenly Father. How did the physical Body of Christ respond? Though Christ ministered to multitudes of people, He still had time for one. He took time to hear their hurts and needs, and provided a healing ministry. Should not the spiritual body of Christ respond today in the same way Christ's physical body responded to the needs of people? As members of Christ Body, we are called to minister to the hurt and pain that dwell within the members of the Lord's Body.

Galatians chapter six verse two states: **"Bear one another's burdens, and thereby fulfill the law of Christ."** How do we fulfill the law of Christ? To begin with, the Church body needs to simply listen to and carry out the will of the Head of the Church, our Lord speaks to us, through His written word, and hearts that are filled with the Holy Spirit. The law of Christ is to love each member of His Body as He loves us. Body members of Christ Body, are called to a full ministry of compassion propelled by hearts filled with God's love. A heart filled love compels us to carry out the will of our Lord, the head of the Church Body. What happens when a member of our physical body is hurt? Why at the mere stump of our toe the body stops, and the hands rush to rub and give comfort to the toe, that the toe might feel better and function again within the body. Should not the Church Body function in the same way? Ministries are not a call for one person to minister the body of our Lord. Christ calls each member of His body to a ministry of His gospel message and His spirit of love. A minister is a person acting as the agent or instrument of another. All who are led by the Holy Word of our Lord, and His Holy Spirit, makes each of them an acting agent, an instrument, a minister of Christ Their Lord. For each member there is a need for them to be ministered to, and to be loved. And each member needs to minister to the need of others in the love of Christ. We need to be ministered to, and we need to minister to others.

God's ministry to us never fails. God will always be there for us, and He will heal us when we reach out to Him in our time of need. How does God bring healing to our hearts and souls? God gives us a ministry. **"Blessed be the God and Father of our Lord Jesus Christ, the Father of compassion and God of all comfort, who comforts us in all our troubles, so that we can comfort those in any trouble with the comfort we ourselves have received from God."** (2 Corinthians' 1:3.) As God ran Phillip along the side of the Ethiopian's chariot, to provide a special ministry for him; God will bring you along the side of someone who has been hurt, as you have been, and He will give to you a healing ministry. A minister friend of mine shared with me that his wife had been abused as a child. The hurt that she carried had an effect on their marriage. One particular week when he was preparing a message on abuse that he was going to present that Sunday morning, his wife told him, that she would like to say something that Sunday. When he had finished his message she came forward and publicly testified for the first time that she had been abused. From that testimony a healing ministry opened up to her. After the service three women came up to her and shared for the first time that they too had been abused. A special ministry began, and a healing process began for her, and for those who came to her. When she came to God with her hurt and special need, God called her to a healing ministry. Are you hurting from some old wounds? God's healing ministry awaits you. When we open up our hearts to God, and to those who need our understanding, then the Lord of compassion and comfort will provide His healing touch.

When we were transferred back to Illinois, Sandra was hired by our friend Tom Smith, as a teacher's aide for kindergartners. This was a great healing process for her. And how greatly blessed were the children who knew her, for Sandra has a love and compassion for little children, and especially for an outcast or hurting child. She is the one who should be writing a book, a book on the heart-warming stories of kindergartners. Sandra and I would also serve in two more churches, where I served as the preacher/minister. This also served to us healing, as we saw many led to Christ through the power of the Lord's gospel message, and the ministry of the Holy Spirit. Through the ministry we also received new friends and lasting relationships bonded in God's love. When we give ourselves unto our Lord's will and serve Him we are blessed. For Jesus our Lord himself said: **"It is more blessed to give than to receive."**(Acts 20:35.)

Jesus also said in Luke 6:38 **"Give and it will be given to you."** I know these words of our Lord to be true through experience, and if you will think back on the blessings of your life, you know the Lord's words to be true in your life too. God's love is not like a bar of soap, soap cleanses you, but the more you use the less you have. God's love will cleanse your heart and the more you use, and share God's love, the more love you receive.

While we have experienced the power of God's love, we have also seen and felt hearts and souls hurt from the lack of God's love being exercised in the Lord's Church Body. Maybe this is one of the reasons I am compelled to write about God's Love. Without God's Love flowing through us we are incomplete for serving God. Our lives and the life of the Lord's Church Body malfunctions for the purpose we are designed, when we fail to exercise God's love in all we do and say. God's Love is the ministry we need, to give and receive. When God's Love is exercised in all we say and do in the Church body, God's Love will propel the Body of Christ into a full and correct ministry that serves the Lord, His Church, and the lost outside of Christ.

Looking back, I will always be thankful for my nephew Kent and his wife Frieda and their two children, Eric and Ali who were close in age to our son Brent. Their home was a few minutes from our home and they shared our grief and they were a comfort to our family. Also, I will never forget and will always be grateful for Kent who took off from work to fly back to Illinois with our son's body. Nor will we ever forget Kelly; she was a ministry of comfort to Sandra, Brent and me. I remember telling her one day that something like this should never happen to a nice Christian young lady like her. Sandra and Kelly still exchange gifts and she will always hold a place of love in our hearts. We haven't seen Kelly in 17 years, but have a picture of Kelly, her husband and their two children and we are happy for her. As I look back, I now know that our son Brent was hurt the worst. During this period of time Brent had to start at two new schools.

He had lost his only brother, and he would lose the function of his parents for some period of time. During this time I had to return to work after one week; I just placed one foot in front of the other. And shortly thereafter Texaco Pipeline transferred me to Port Arthur; I was driving 90 miles to work and trying to find a home. Also, during this period of time, Sandra was under a Doctor's care. We couldn't see during that time Brent needed some out side help. While I can't conjure words to describe the depths of grief we had, I can't imagine or describe the amount of hurt that our son was receiving and enduring, and much of the time on his own. My heart yet today weighs heavy for my son Brent and what happened to him. And at times I wrestle with the will of God.

THE THREE WILLS OF GOD.

God's definite will.-- I understand God's definite will and I love the Lord's definite will. His will is good for us and for all those around us. To walk as Jesus walked, to walk in His love and kindness, and with the gentleness and humbleness of the Heart of Christ, made God's will, perfect for our lives, and for the lives around us.

God's ultimate will.-- I also know and understand God's ultimate will, and I love His ultimate will, and look forward to the time when our Lord welcomes us home. Where we will join Him in the richest of His Kingdom, where no sin nor heartache will exist throughout eternity.

God's permissive will.-- But until that day, I guess I will never fully understand God's permissive will. I know our Father created us as free will agents giving us the right to make right moral choices, and if we have the right to choose right moral choices, we must also have the right to make wrong moral choices. And we must know good consequences follow good choices, and bad consequences follow bad choices. Also God's permissive will allows us time, to accept, or reject, "God's love for us." This much of God's permissive will for this probationary period of time in which He has allotted us to live in I believe I understand. But many things I don't understand. To name a few, why do innocent children have to be hurt who did nothing wrong, and had no choice in the consequences that brought them pain and suffering? Why do innocent children receive abuse? Why should any parent out live their child? Why do innocent children lose their brother and their parents? I know that isn't in God's will, but His permissive will allows these things to happen during this life time. I think about Stephen who was such a dynamic young man, and lover of the Lord, who had so much to offer to the Lord's Kingdom, and to the world. Yet God in his permissive will allowed him to be killed.

For now and for the things I don't understand, I take consolation in what I do know, **"that in all things God works for the good of those who love him."** (Romans' 8:28). Stephen in his day of tribulation God revealed to him His glory and the glory of heaven that awaited him. I also know God loves us, and His will for our life is good, pleasing, and perfect for our lives; God's will for our lives cannot be improved upon. Like a perfect golf stance, grip, and swing, at first it goes against what we would naturally do. But once in place it will deliver our goals for a better life. God's will in our life delivers our lives into a better life! The perfect will of God will transform our lives into our lord's love, His complete joy, and perfect peace. We can't miss "God's love for us," for God's love surrounds us.

GODS LOVE FOR US, SURROUNDS US, AND FILLS US.

God's love for us is a full and complete love that surrounds us, and fills us in every sense of our beings. We are the children of the Heavenly Father, who created us for His love. The Heavenly Father has cast His love upon us, around us, and within us.

God surrounds us with His love, in the beauty of His creation. We see the beauty of God's love for us in the rising and setting of the sun that He put in place. And He gives us a warm cup of coffee to take in the beauty of the colors He paints at sunrise and sunset, color that brings warmth to our hearts. For no human hands can capture the colors and beauty that God's loving hand paints for us each day. And when clouds arise and storms come our way, in time the sun will reappear, and then God paints in the sky a beautiful rainbow to reassure us of His love for us. Then in the cool of the night when we take time to look up, after a long and tiring day, God puts us to rest as we gaze into the stars that God's love has put in place for us. Everything seems to fall into its proper perspective, as we gaze into the vastness of the universe. We see the greatness of God, and "Gods love for us" that brings peace to our hearts.

Throughout our daily journeys God's love surrounds us with the beauty of His love. When we see the beauty of flowers springing forth and trees budding out into the air, we see and smell the freshness and beauty of God's love surrounding us. We see and smell the freshness of His raindrops that cleanses the air and

Chapter One: "God's Love For Us"

gives growth to the beauty of the creation He created for us. We see and feel the beauty of each snowflake designed by our Creator's Hand falling softly around us, and we feel the cool moisture He places in each flake. Throughout our life's journey God surrounds our senses with His love. We can see, hear, smell, touch and feel, God's love surrounding our lives each day.

God also sends into our lives hearts filled with His love. Hearts filled with God's love carrying words of kindness, and words of comfort, bringing us words of encouragement that spurs our lives on to love and good deeds. We also receive God's love in arms of loving hearts that reach out to hold us. In loving hearts, God sends His love. In every waking day, when we open our eye's to see and know God's love, His love is surrounding us to warm our hearts through the beauty of His nature, and the love and beauty of the Children of the Heavenly King that God sends our way.

When we place all our hope in God, through good times and bad times, through laughter and tears, our hope in God will never disappoint us, nor fail us. For, "God's love for us" will fill our hearts with His preserving love when we reach out to Him in faith. Roman's chapter five verse five makes this statement: "**and hope does not disappoint, because the love of God has been poured out within our hearts through the Holy Spirit who was given to us.**" The love of God within our heart pumps energy and strength into our lives. God's love within us overcomes and delivers us to times of joy and refreshing, as we travel through our boundaries of time. And then "God's love for us," reaches out to us, and into us, beyond the bounds of time, from the time we receive Jesus, God's gift of love, we will know "God's love for us," God's love around us, and God's love within us, and we will live in God's perfect love throughout eternity.

We receive God's gift of love within us when we choose to open the eye's and doors of our hearts, to look upon Jesus, and receive Him into our hearts as lord and Savior of our lives. Jesus is God's gift of love, joy, and peace for our lives.

JESUS IS THE WAY TO GOD'S LOVE AND FREEDOM.

Jesus said: **"I am the way, and the truth, and the life; no one comes to the Father, but through Me."** (John 14:6). Jesus is not one way among many, he is <u>the way</u>, to a true love relationship with our Heavenly Father, and for the blessings God has prepared for those who make Jesus Lord and Savior of their lives. Lord and Savior go hand in hand; they cannot be separated. Many want to have Jesus as their Savior but do not want to make him Lord of their lives. We found in Colossians chapter one verse nineteen **"For it was the Father's good pleasure for all the fullness to dwell in Him,(Jesus) and through Him to reconcile all things to Himself, having made peace through the blood of the cross; through Him."** Jesus must be the Lord of our lives, if we are to know the fullness of our Heavenly Father and the blessings of life. For Jesus is the totality of God with all his powers and attributes. When we choose to make Jesus Lord of our lives by submitting our lives unto His will, then Jesus chooses to be our Savior. Jesus is the way to "God's love for us," God's love is a love willing to die for our sins, that separates us from Him. Sin constitutes going against the will of the Heavenly Father whose will seeks the best interest and welfare for all His children. As long as we choose to live in our sins, we remain as rebellious children of God, who are at war against the will of our Heavenly Father. Sin separates us from the fellowship and love of our Heavenly Father. Our sin also leaves a trail of tears, from broken homes, broken hearts, verbal and physical abuse, broken trusts, and broken dreams. The wages of sin leaves bound up hearts and chained souls, chains that we cannot break! Our hearts and souls are imprisoned by sin and bound for death!

What can save us from this horrible imprisonment of our souls and sentence of death? For every sin that we have ever committed, and we have all sinned, has been directed against our Heavenly Father. Every time we sin against the objects of God's love, we sin against our Heavenly Father. What are the objects of God's love? Every person we meet is the object of God's love, for we each are the objects of our Heavenly Father's love. Therefore, all the words, actions, and deeds we direct toward one another outside of our Father's love that brings hurt and pain to another, are directed to our Heavenly Father who loves us. He feels our hurt and pain that result from sin.

It takes a loving mother or father to understand the Heavenly Father's love. When the child of a loving mother or father comes home hurting from the words or deeds of another directed at them, their hurt radiates into the heart of their loving mother and father and they feel their pain. Our Heavenly Father sees and feels the hurt and pain that sin brings to both the offender and the victim. Our Heavenly Father's boundless love for us, reaches out beyond human comprehension to heal and free His children of the cause and effect of sin upon them and within them. And our God will accomplish this through the greatest display of love the world has ever known. Our Heavenly Father accomplishes His desire to free us from sin and reconcile us unto Himself as children of the Heavenly King by making peace through Jesus' blood shed on the cross. (Colossians 1:20).

That we might see and understand better the love and depths of God's love and plan of salvation to free us from the wages of sin, let us look intently into the Revelations of Jesus Christ that God gave unto Him, to give and show to His servants. A revealing look into Revelations chapter five verses one through ten reveals to us why it took God's only begotten Son to shed his blood, and die for our sins upon the cruel cross of Calvary.

WHY GOD SHED THE BLOOD OF HIS ONE AND ONLY BEGOTTEN SON!

"I saw in the right hand of Him who sat on the throne a book written inside and on the back, sealed up with seven seals. And I saw a mighty angel proclaiming in a loud voice, who is worthy to break the seals and open the scroll? But no one in heaven or on earth or under the earth could open the scroll or even look inside it. I wept and wept because no one was found who was worthy to open the scroll or look inside. Then one of the elders said to me, "Do not weep! See, the Lion of the tribe of Judah, the root of David, has triumphed. He is able to open the scroll and its seven seals."

Then I saw a Lamb, looking as if he had been slain, standing in the center of the throne, encircled by the four living creatures and the elders, He had seven horns and seven eyes, which are the seven spirits of God sent out into all the earth. He came and took the scroll from the right hand of Him who sat on the throne. And when He had taken it the four living creatures and the twenty-four elders fell down before the Lamb. Each one had a harp and they were holding golden bowls full of incense, which are the prayers of the saints."

And they sang a new song, saying,

"Worthy are you to take the book and to break its seals; for you were slain, and purchased for God with Your blood men from every tribe and tongue and people and nation.

"You have made them to be a kingdom and priests to our God; and they will reign upon the earth." (Revelation's 5:1-10)

Chapter One: "God's Love For Us"

Looking into a part of God's revelation of Jesus Christ that was given to Jesus, and Jesus made it known by sending His angel to His servant John, and John recorded what he saw.

The Revelation of Jesus Christ was recorded that we might see and gain the knowledge of Jesus our Lord, God's salvation plan for us, and God's love for us. What do we see revealed to us of our Heavenly Father and of our Lord and Savior who loves us? We see the following:

- We see God ruling from His throne and in His right hand is a scroll written on both sides indicating the complete word and will of God.

- We see a mighty angel proclaiming in a loud voice that all in heaven and earth might hear, "Who is worthy to break the seals and open the scroll?" But no one in heaven or earth, or under the earth, was able or worthy to open God's plan for man and carry it out.

- We see John weeping and weeping, for it seemed we would not receive the salvation plan of God, His abiding love, or eternal life within us. All seemed lost.

- We see one of the elders say to John, "Do not weep! See, the Lion of the tribe of Judah, the root of David, has triumphed." For Christ is able and worthy to carry out God's redeeming plans for his children.

- We see John turning probably expecting to see a lion, but to his surprise he sees a Lamb standing in the center of the throne, looking as if it had been slain. He had seven horns and seven eyes indicating the complete authority and power of God. We see the prayers of the saints being answered. We see Jesus the slain and perfect Lamb of God take the scroll to carry out the Heavenly Father's will.

- We see in heaven a glorious song burst forth "worthy is the Lamb," for Christ, the lamb of God, has purchased us to be a kingdom, and priests to God, through the shedding of His blood and the power of His Spirit.

The big and true picture we see here is that the will and mind of God rules. This is the main headline we need to place in our minds, all other headlines we see and read are secondary compared to: "God is in control." We also see that God's salvation plan for man, and Christ's Kingdom came not by force, but rather by submission of the Lamb of God unto His Father's will. And we also can only enter into our lord's kingdom by submission unto our Lord's Word and Spirit. The power of God's Spirit of love enters into humble contrite hearts that are willing to submit their lives unto Christ and accept Jesus as their Lord and Savior. God's salvation, eternal life, and life more abundantly, only comes to us by Jesus blood and righteousness.

THE GREATEST NEWS THE WORLD HAS EVER RECEIVED!

How did "God's love for us" reach out to us and free us from the bondage of sin, and the penalty of death? God's love reaches out to us in our hopeless despair, through his one and only begotten Son, whom God sends to free us from the sin that separates us from our Heavenly Father and His gift of life. The greatest news we have ever received came in one sentence, from the worlds greatest messenger, Jesus our Lord and Savior: **"For God so loved the world, that He gave His only begotten Son, that whoever believes in Him should not perish, but have eternal life."** (John 3:16). As ambassadors and ministers for our Lord, which all His disciples are, we can carry no greater message to others from our King Jesus than His message found in John 3:16. For to know that God loves you, and is willing to free you from sin and death, there is no greater news. Jesus, God's son, came to live for us, die for us, and live within us.

To begin to know and understand the depths of "God's love for us," we must gaze upon the cross of Calvary and look to what led Jesus there, and why Jesus had to die and shed His blood on the cross of Calvary, and how did the shedding of His blood make peace? I think we first need to understand that outside of Christ, the love and the will of our Heavenly Father, we stand as rebellious children at war with our Heavenly Father. God sees us in our rebellious stand dying in our sins. Then God's love reaches out to us, His rebellious and lost children, in a love beyond degree and comprehension of our minds. Our Heavenly Father's love for us sheds the blood of His one and only Begotten Son, on the cross of Calvary.

We can only begin to explain and understand why God shed His Sons blood on the cross at Calvary. But as we do let us see in the shed blood, the love of our Heavenly Father for us, and the love of our Lord and Savior for us, that was poured out at Calvary. To know "God's love for us," we must look to the cross of Jesus at Calvary.

God's Blood Covenants!

We know by the Holy Scriptures that God deals with us through covenants. God's covenants are agreements and promises between the Heavenly Father and His children. We have no part in making up the agreement. God writes the covenant. Our part is to acknowledge and keep our part of the agreement of God's covenants, the good news is that God's conditional covenant comes with God's great love and blessings for us when we keep our part of the agreement. Although some of the covenants of God are strictly unconditional, they amount to a promise or act of mere favor from God to His people, for instance, the assurance given by God after the flood, that a like judgement would not be repeated. And when we see the beautiful rainbow God places before us after the rain, we are reminded of His covenant, and that God always keeps His word and covenant. But God's covenants that are ratified by blood are conditional, we have a part to keep.

For our understanding of God's blood covenants let us begin at the Passover. When God decided to free His people from the bondage of the Egyptians, He made a covenant with His people ratified by blood. The Lord instructed Moses and Aaron to tell the whole community of Israel that they were to pick out unblemished lambs, and they were to slaughter the unblemished lambs at twilight. Then they were instructed in detail how to cook and prepare the meat and how to eat it. They were instructed to take the blood of the slain lamb and put it on the tops and sides of the door frames of the houses where they ate the lambs. This was called the Lord's Passover, for that night when the Lord passed judgement upon Egypt and their gods, God would pass over the peoples houses that were sealed and protected by the blood of the lamb. They were further instructed this would be a lasting ordinance, and when they entered the promise land they were to observe the ceremony. When their children asked them what the ceremony meant they were to testify to them how the Lord had spared them, for they were protected by the seal of the blood of the Lamb. For further understanding of God's blood covenants we find this instruction of the Lord, given to Moses to tell God's people in Leviticus 17:11. **"For the life of the creature is in the blood, and I have given it to you to make atonement for yourselves on the altar; it is the blood that makes atonement for one's life."** This word of God is teaching us that blood makes atonement, and the atonement involves the substitution of life for life. Why did God shed the life blood of His one and only begotten Son? Because Jesus was the only perfect unblemished sacrificial lamb whose life might be substituted, for the atonement of our sins. **"And according to the law, one may almost say, all things are cleansed with blood, and without the shedding of blood there is no forgiveness."** (Hebrew's 9:22) **"The blood of Jesus His Son, purifies us from all sin."** (1 John 1:7). We have received forgiveness of our sins by the redeeming blood of God's Son, Jesus our Lord. All praises are to be given unto the Heavenly Father and Jesus the Son, for their love and sacrifices that we might have life, and life abundantly.

Why did Jesus, the perfect one without sin, have to shed His blood and die for us? Jesus was the only one worthy! Jesus was God's unblemished Lamb, the righteousness of God! Again, why did Jesus have to die and shed His blood on the cruel cross at Calvary? First of all, He did not have to, Jesus' love for the Heavenly Father and His love for us, propelled him to sacrifice Himself in our place, and receive God's wrath for our sins that we might have life. The Lamb of God gave His life that we might have life. It took the purity of Jesus Life Blood to atone for our sins.

God's Holy Word in first Peter chapter two verse twenty four, gave one of the best exclamations of why Jesus in His love for us, chose to die for us. **"Jesus himself bore our sins in His body on the cross, so that we might die to sin and live to righteousness: for by His wounds you were healed."**

JESUS SACRIFICED HIS LIFE BLOOD FOR ALL THE WORLDS!

For all peoples before and after the cross Jesus shed His life blood. **"God presented Him as a sacrifice of atonement, through faith in His blood. He did this to demonstrate His justice, because in His forbearance He had left the sins before Him unpunished."**(Romans 3:25). Before the cross of Jesus, God was forbearing the sins of His people who placed their faith and trust in Him. God was not remitting their sins but only forbearing their sins until there became an adequate atonement for sin. God being a righteous and just God had to fully punish sin. And God being a God of love desired to fully forgive the sins of His children who cried out to Him in faith. Until the blood of Jesus shed upon the cross, God could not fully punish, nor fully forgive us of our sins. God's perfect sacrificial Lamb, while upon the cross of Calvary, received God's full wrath and punishment for all the sins, of all who place their faith and trust in God. And through the shedding of Jesus atoning blood, God's perfect sacrificial Lamb, God could fully forgive the sins of all people who placed their faith in Him, and gave Him their love before and after the cross. All people who had placed their faith and love in God, before the cross, looked forward to the Messiah, for salvation from their sins. All people who place their faith and trust in the blood of Jesus, giving Him their love and obedience, look back through the blood of the cross to the Messiah for salvation from their sins. **"He is the atoning sacrifice for our sins, and not only for ours but also for the sins of the whole world."**(1John 2:2).

What a blessing is ours who live on this side of the cross. We have seen the full punishment for our sins, and know the full forgiveness of our sins through the atoning blood of Jesus. Not only do we have the knowledge of the full forgiveness of our sins, we have a High Priest who knows our hearts, and pleads our case before the almighty God. For Jesus entered into the Most Holy Place, heaven itself, through His atoning blood as our High Priest forever.

"When Christ came as high priest of the good things that are already here, He went through the greater and more perfect tabernacle that is not man-made, that is to say not part of this creation.

He did not enter by the means of the blood of goats and calves; but He entered the Most Holy Place once for all by His own blood, having obtained eternal redemption. The blood of goats and bulls and the ashes of a heifer sprinkled on those who are ceremonially unclean sanctify them so that they are outwardly clean.

How much more, then, will the blood of Christ, who through the eternal spirit offered Himself unblemished to God, cleanse our consciences from acts that lead to death, so that we may serve the living God!"(Hebrew's 9:11-14).

How much greater we should love and serve the Lord our God, since we have full forgiveness of our sins. And since we have Jesus to approach to receive mercy and grace in our times of need as our High Priest.

WHAT MUST WE DO TO COMPLETE GOD'S BLOOD COVENANT OF LOVE?

God's covenant of love for us is a covenant forever, sealed and paid for by the blood of God's only begotten Son. Part of God's Covenant of love for us was unconditional, and part is conditional. What God's love did at Calvary through the love of Jesus was unconditional. Jesus Christ shed His blood and died for all on the cross at Calvary. Whether we accept it, or reject it, Jesus, God's Son, shed His blood and died for us that we might be forgiven of our sins, and be reconciled to our Heavenly Father as his child throughout eternity. But the acceptance of God's Gift of life, and the forgiveness of our sins is conditional. God made the agreement but we must meet the agreement of Jesus shed blood for us. How do we accept God's forgiveness of sins and the gift of life? What shall we do? This was the question of three thousand hearts and souls pierced by the Holy Spirit after they had heard the gospel message of Jesus Christ, preached for the first time by Peter on the day of Pentecost. Why would it be Peter to give the first gospel message of Jesus Christ for the first time? And why would Peter have the answer to pierced hearts crying out what shall we do?

The answers to these questions are found in Jesus' statements to Peter right after Peter had just answered Jesus question of "who do you say that I am?" Peter replied, **"You are the Christ, the Son of the living God."** Then Jesus makes this statement to Peter: **"Blessed are you, Simon son of Jonah, for this was not revealed to you by man, but by my Father in heaven. And I tell you that you are Peter, and on this rock I will build my** church, and the gates of hades will not overcome it. **<u>I will give you the keys of the kingdom of heaven;</u> whatever you bind on earth will be bound in heaven, and whatever you loose on earth will be loosed in heaven."** (Matthew 16:16-19.) And now that we have the answer to those questions, what is Peter's answer to the question of three thousand pierced hearts crying out after hearing what Jesus had done for them, **"What shall we do?"** Peter gives to them the key to the kingdom of God, and to all thereafter, who cries out "what shall we do?" after hearing the gospel message of Jesus Christ love and sacrifice for their sins. Peter's answer, the key that gives us entrance into the Kingdom of God, was given after this universal plea of those whose hearts are pierced by the message of the cross **"When the people heard this, they were pierced to the heart, and said to Peter and the rest of the Apostles, "Brothers, what shall we do?"**(Acts 2:37). Then Peter using the keys of the kingdom of heaven, which Jesus gave him replied, **"Repent, and let each of you be baptized in the name of Jesus Christ for the forgiveness of your sins; And you shall receive the gift of the Holy Spirit. For the promise is for you and your children, and for all who are far off, as many as the Lord our God shall call to Himself."** (Acts 2:38-39)

JESUS COMES TO US, AND WE COME TO JESUS BY THE WAY OF THE CROSS!

By the way of the cross, Jesus represents God's great sacrificial gift for our forgiveness and reunion with Him. A little boy was once asked, "How do you define forgiveness?" The little boy replied: "It's like stepping on and crushing a flower, and after the flower is crushed it continues to give off more fragrance." One day the beautiful Rose of Sharon carrying the aroma of God's forgiving love, was crushed upon the cross of Calvary, and the fragrance of God's forgiveness dispersed from God's Rose of Sharon and covered the entire world.

All who enter the Kingdom of Christ must come by the way of the cross. Jesus said: "When I am lifted up on the cross at Calvary I will draw all people to myself." Jesus said, **"When you have lifted up the Son of Man, then you will know that I am the one I claim to be, and that I do nothing on my own but speak just what my Father has taught Me. The One who sent Me is with Me; He has not left Me alone, for I always do what pleases Him."**(John 8:28 & 29.) **"But I, when I am lifted up from the earth, will draw all men to Myself."**(John 12:32.) Only when we stop and gaze into the cross of Jesus, do we begin to see the kindness and fullness of "God's love for us." God's kindness toward us, leads us to repentance. And the love of Christ compels our hearts to commit our lives to Jesus in Christian baptism. Christian baptism is a plea to God for a clear conscience through God's forgiveness of sins. Christian baptism is a public statement that we are dying and being immersed into Christ: Then symbolic of being born again, we break through the water, to arise from our death in Christ, to walk in a newness of life in Christ, claiming Jesus as Lord and Savior of our life.

Then having received the promise of God's gifts of love and life within us through the Holy Spirit, we put on Christ, denying ourselves, and pick up our cross, following, loving, and serving our Lord and Savior through His Word and Spirit of love. A full committed life in Christ brings the full blessings of God. To fully know and receive "God's love for us," calls for us to be fully committed to Jesus, as our Lord and Savior.

And now to increase our view of "God's love us," and the price that God's love paid for us, maybe we should look into the prophecy of Isaiah in chapter fifty three written about 700 to 680-year's B.C.

The following scripture has sometimes been called the Old Testament gospel of Jesus Christ.

Chapter One: "God's Love For Us"

The prophecy of God's great sacrifice and love for us!

"He grew up before him like a tender shoot,
and a root out of dry ground.
He had no beauty or majesty to attract us to Him,
nothing in His appearance that we should desire Him.
He was despised and rejected by men,
a man of sorrows, and familiar with suffering.
Like one from whom men hide their faces
He was despised and we esteemed Him not.

Surely He took our infirmities
and carried our sorrows,
yet we considered Him stricken by God,

smitten by Him, and afflicted.
But He was pierced for our transgressions,

He was crushed for our iniquities;
the punishment that brought us
peace was upon Him,
and by His wounds we are healed.
We all, like sheep have gone astray,
each of us has turned to his own
way;
and the Lord has laid on Him
the iniquity of us all.
He was oppressed and afflicted,
yet He did not open His mouth;
He was led like a lamb to the
slaughter,
and as sheep before her shearers is
silent,
so He did not open His mouth.
By oppression and judgement He was
taken away.
And who can speak of His
descendants?
For He was cut off from the land of the
living;
for the transgressions of my people
He was stricken.
He was assigned a grave with the
wicked,
and with the rich in His death,
though He had done no violence,

nor was any deceit in His mouth.
Yet it was the Lord's will to crush
Him and cause Him to suffer,
and though the Lord makes His life
a guilt offering,
He will see His offspring and prolong
His days,
and the will of the Lord will
prosper in His hand.
After the suffering of His soul,

He will see the light of life and be
satisfied
by His knowledge my righteous
servant will justify many,
and He will bear their iniquities,
therefore I will give Him a portion
among the great,
and He will divide the spoils with
the strong,
because He has poured out His life unto
death,

And was numbered with the
transgressors.
For He bore the sin of many,
And made intercession for the
Transgressors."

(Isaiah chapter 53)

God gives us another view of Jesus our Lord through His prophet Isaiah. The descriptive writing of Isaiah removes us from our comfort zone of viewing Jesus through nativity sets and beautiful paintings of Jesus on the cross. God through Isaiah exposes us to a full heart wrenching view of "God's love for us," carried out in the life of Jesus. And maybe that is why many prefer just beautiful little glimpses of the life and cross of Jesus, rather than the full view of the life and cross of Jesus. For a full view of the life of Jesus reaches deep into our hearts, which calls for and produces life changing views of our hearts and minds. The life and the cross of Jesus will awaken our slumbering souls to the complete reality of God, and "God's love for us." When we take a full view of the life of Jesus, we no longer just see footprints of God's love and existence. In the life and cross of Jesus we see a full-blown exposure of the existence of God and all His attributes, including "God's love for us." In the life, death, burial, and resurrection of Jesus, God's Son, God, has given us the most proven, significant, historical fact ever given to mankind. And beyond the pages of history written in ink, God writes upon our hearts with the blood of His only begotten Son, His love for us. In Jesus, God fully exposes His existence and His love for us.

Can anyone fully comprehend God? The existence of a Sovereign, Transcendent, Infinite, Eternal God is incomprehensible. But even without the knowledge of Jesus, our existence through the creation of an eternal God is more comprehensible than any of our man-made theories of our existence, which always begins with matter. Who can even begin to understand eternity? In our world of beginnings and endings we have a hard time of comprehending eternity. But, eternal matter or eternal God, are the only choices of our beginning and of our existence, both are incomprehensible. The choice of a beginning from existing matter, and a self existing universe, (which by the way is being taught in our schools) is far more incomprehensible than creation by an eternal God, especially when we consider the scientific law of "cause and effect." Order and complexity doesn't just happen! There must be a programmer for the existence of order and complexity. Therefore creation can be the only logical answer to the order and complexity of the universe and of our existence. And in that answer there must exist an infinite eternal God, who is also omnipotent, having the power to call the universe into being.

A good friend of mine down in Texas, Larry Skero, once said to me: "Jim, sometimes we go down so deep, we come up shallow." I believe Larry is especially right when we try to comprehend the existence of God. But! God's existence bursts through the surface of our hearts and minds when we fully view the life, and the cross, and the resurrection of Jesus. When we see Jesus, our hearts and minds see the existence and fullness of "God's love for us."

LIVING IN THE 3-DIMENSIONS OF GOD'S GIFT OF LOVE!

In Jesus we are not only free from our sin that imprisons and chains our spirits, Jesus frees us from the penalty of our sins, which is death! And He gives us life and freedom! "God's love for us," goes beyond the cross of Jesus. God provides the empowerment, through the Holy Spirit, to thrust our lives into the full dimensions of His love, when our hearts are energized at the birth and resurrection of Christ into our hearts. We are born again, when the Bright and Morning Star rises into the darkness of our hearts, and minds, He lights up our lives, setting our hearts aglow with the Spirit of God's love.

God sent us His love and His very being wrapped in swaddling clothes. When we choose to unwrap the greatest Gift, the world has ever been given, we see Jesus. But, to accept and receive God's gift of Jesus into our lives, we must give Jesus the seat of honor in our hearts and minds, making King Jesus King of our lives. When we receive God's precious gift of Jesus, we find the following gifts of God's love all wrapped up in Jesus.

- A true love relationship with our Heavenly Father!

- Jesus living within us, we will never live alone, nor be forsaken!

- Jesus' complete joy dwelling within us!

- God's peace in our lives!

- Truth that sets our spirits free!

- In Jesus we have a more abundant life, and life complete!

- Eternal life!

All the above and more are gifts of God's love for us when we receive Jesus, God's gift of love, into our hearts as Lord of our lives.

Why should "God's love for us," be chapter one in this book? And why should "God's love for you" be chapter one in your heart and life? Because our future is wrapped up and determined by our past and present belief of our origin. To know we were created by an omnipotent, holy, loving God, for a divine purpose and destiny, must give into our life's purpose, and motivation, and propel our lives into a future of love and good works. We must know that God loves us, in order for our lives to advance upward into the dimensions of God's love and more abundant life. We can't enter into the full dimensions of God's love, until we know "God's love for us" and God's love dwelling in us. God's love dwelling in us is the first step and prerequisite for completing God's love and completing our lives.

The second step into the dimensions of God's complete love, is "Our Love for God." For God's love to be complete we must learn to return the indwelling spirit of God's love back unto God. For a true love relationship to exist between ourselves and our Heavenly Father, God's love must be reciprocal. In order to complete the second step into the full dimensions of God's love, we necessarily must have God's love dwelling within us, and return our love to God.

The third dimensional step into the complete dimension of God's love is "our love for one another." To complete God's love we must learn to cast God's indwelling love within us, upon the objects of God's love. For God's love to complete us, and function properly in our lives, God's love must flow into our hearts, and flow out of our lives, first and foremost up to God, and then out to one another.

To reach the divine purpose and destiny of our life, and to know life in its fullness it is imperative that we know the existence of God, and live in the 3- dimensions of Gods love.

VIEWING "GOD'S LOVE FOR US!"

Viewing the Garden of Gethsemane!

A further look into "God's love for us," reveals that "God's love for us" drew salvation's plan, and the salvation plan of God was carried out by our Lord and Savior's love for the Father and for us. For another view of Gods love, let our hearts and minds view Jesus in the Garden of Gethsemane. We see our Lord's soul in distress near the point of death. We see Him praying fervently. Sweat is falling from our Lord like great drops of blood. An Angel comes to attend our Lord and Savior giving Him strength that He might endure the road that lay ahead of Him. Jesus is praying that the cup of pain and agony that He must drink to free us from sin and death might somehow be removed.

Have you ever wondered why Jesus returned twice to look upon His disciples faces during this great time of agony in His soul? Did He see your face and my face that day? Was it to see our weakness, our hopeless state of broken hearts and dying bodies ravaged by sin? Was it a look of compassion, seeing our desperate need of His love and sacrifice? Was it a look upon our face to reassure our Savior of our desperate need of His dying love and sacrifice? Was it a final look by our Savior, upon each of God's lost children's faces that touched our Lords' heart and caused Him to know and say they are worth all Our love and sacrifice Heavenly Father? **"My Father, if it is possible, let this cup pass from me; yet not as I will, but as you will."**(Matthew 26:39). That is one measure of "God's love for us."

Viewing the Road to Calvary!

And now for a further look at "God's love for us," a love that reaches beyond human comprehension, we see God's only begotten Son under the weight of a wooden cross, climbing up the road to Mount Calvary. That road is my road, and your road that our Savior is climbing, and the cross our Lord is carrying is our cross! Their spitting on our Lord and Savior, mocking and laughing at the Holy One, Jesus is receiving and bearing the humiliation, for our sins. Our Lord, under our cross bears our stripes upon His back; He has taken our beating. God's wrath for our sins is falling on our Lord's body that was my road and your road of pain and humiliation our Savior walked for us. He was God's perfect sacrificial Lamb, for only our Lord was worthy to pay the price for the sin of debt we owed. Have you ever seen a greater love and sacrifice? Have you ever been loved so? We love you, Lord Jesus!

The Price Jesus Paid for us at Mount Calvary!

And now we look upon our Lord and Savior, God's Son, upon the cruel cross of Calvary. For none of us can ever see the measure of God's love, and the measure of the value God has placed on each of our lives, until we stop and view the cross of Jesus, and take it into our hearts. As we look to the cross, we see our Lord as He hangs in suffering anguish between heaven and earth, beaten beyond recognition. We see our Lord hanging there despised and rejected by earth and forsaken by heaven.

Chapter One: "God's Love For Us"

Never has a human life been in such a desolate state, never has love paid such a price. We hear him now, God's perfect Lamb being <u>slain</u> and crying out **"My God, My God, why hast Thou forsaken Me?"** (Mark 15:34). Imagine the love and heartbreak of the Heavenly Father for His one and only begotten Son, now unable to look upon His Son whose body is filled with our sins, as He bears the wrath of God for all the sins of the world. For our Lord's love for the Father, and for His love for each of us, Jesus is bearing each of our sins in His body on that cruel cross of agony, humiliation, desolation, and pain. As we look upon the extreme physical pain that our Lord suffered in our place, we can only image the pain and heartbreak that He is suffering in his heart and soul. He who never knew sin, now is bearing the hurt and pain for all the sins of the world, we can only imagine. For, no one but our Lord and Savior has ever experienced total absence from our Heavenly Father. Try to imagine the holiness and purity of our Lord Jesus, and of our Lord Jesus always being one in the Father, never knowing sin, now bearing the sins of the world, paying the penalty for the ones who drove the nails in his hands, forsaken by his Heavenly Father. Listen, if we can, to the agony of God's sacrificial Lamb being slain and crying out for His Heavenly Father. Oh! Are we worth that price? No greater love for you and me has ever been displayed. "God's love for us" must reach deep into our hearts as we view the agony of the cross. God's love reaches beyond our comprehension, when we look to the cross and see that our Heavenly Father would sacrifice His one and only begotten Son. And that God's Son was willing to bear our sins, and suffer the penalty of God's wrath for our sins, that we might be redeemed as Children of the Heavenly Father. At the cross we see the dying love of our Lord and Savior, a love willing to bear our sins and our penalty of death, that we might share in His Kingdom, and become Children of the Heavenly King through His atoning blood.

"GOD'S LOVE FOR US" WAS MEASURED AT CALVARY!

Do you see the greatness of our worth and value? Our full worth and value were measured at Calvary, when the fullness of God's love was cast out for you and me through the blood of God's one and only begotten Son, which makes our value immeasurable. Jesus gave His heart for you and me at Calvary. When the soldier's spear pierced through the sac surrounding the heart of Jesus, blood and water gushed out from our Saviors broken heart. Jesus gave His heart and life blood for us at Calvary, that our sins might be washed away. How valuable we are! How loved we are! What makes our worth so valuable beyond measure? Our worth and value were measured by "God's love for us," which came to us through the heart of Jesus.

"For God so loved the world that he gave his one and only begotten Son that whoever believes in him should not perish, but have eternal life."(John 3:16). God's love for us is the greatest news we will ever receive, and the greatest news we will ever share! God's Son lived for us, died for us, and lives for us, to show us the way unto the Heavenly Father. A relationship with the Heavenly Father will bring to us, God's love, His joy, and His peace, that we might have life and have it more abundantly! This is "God's love for us!" And what great and immeasurable value God placed on you and me, when the heart of God was poured out for you and me at Calvary.

Chapter One: "God's Love For Us"

Our Heavenly Father sent us His love, His gift of life, His spirit of joy, and spirit of peace all wrapped up in swaddling clothes, God's Son. We receive God's Gift of life and love within us, when we accept Jesus as Lord and Savior of our lives.

If God is willing to die for you, God is willing to live within you, if you are willing to die to Him and live for Him. How? By turning your heart and soul over to Jesus, making Him Lord of your life! Jesus promises to those who love and obey Him that He will enter into their hearts that we might not only know "God's Love for us," but that we might also know the enabling and empowering spirit of God's love living in us. Only you can open your heart to whom and what you choose. And that is a good thing. But the greatest thing you can ever do, is to open your heart's door to Jesus and let Him come into your heart, to love and live for you. The greatest power the world has ever known was displayed at Calvary when God's Son hung between heaven and earth. The Kingdom of God never came by force, but rather by the full submission of our Lord and Savior unto His Father's will. And the earthly Kingdom of God today moves not by the will and agenda's of man, but rather by full submission unto the will and agenda of the Heavenly Father. Following the example of our Lord and Savior, we are enabled and empowered by the Spirit of our Lord, into a full submission unto His will. The kingdom of God came, and the Kingdom of God moves, through complete submission unto the power of God's Word and Spirit.

"God's love for us" flows out to us through the words and life of Jesus. Through the grace gift of God's one and only begotten Son, God's love flowed from Calvary. And all who choose to receive God's greatest gift of grace must kneel before the cross of Jesus, God's gift of grace, and be washed in the atoning blood of Christ. Jesus is the gushing spring of God's love that fills the thirst of all who choose to drink of Him. All who robe their selves in Jesus, accepting and honoring Him as King and Lord of their lives, God fills and overflows their hearts with His love. And they too, the hearts of Jesus, become gushing springs of God's love. "God's love for us" is completed when the Spirit of Christ love lives in us and through us.

There has been a lot written about, and spoken on, "Its not about me." But, on the cross at Calvary, when God poured out the fullness of His love, and shed the blood of His one and only begotten Son upon that cross, it was all about you! And all for you! When we look to the cross of Calvary, we see upon the cross, the fullness of "God's love for us." "God's love for us" expresses His kindness, His grace and mercy toward us, to draw us, His children near unto Him, and into His caring arms of protective love. God's love is "all about you." God's love reaches out to you that you might be redeemed as a child of the Heavenly King. When you are a child of the Heavenly King, you are made complete through the riches of our Lord's Spirit of love, that God places in you. The entrance into the riches of God's glory is provided to us by, "God's love for us." Do not let circumstances rule and shape your life, let the Spirit of Christ, and the love of God, rule and shape your life.

If you have received anything from this chapter on "Gods love for us," that may have benefitted you in your spiritual quest, then all the glories are to God, from whom all good things come.

At the end of each chapter will be some thought provoking questions which may help us in our spiritual quest in knowing God, and the power of His Spirit of Love. Our answers to the questions should be attained through the Holy Scriptures and the Holy Spirit.

"GODS LOVE FOR US!"
Questionnaire

#-1.   What is the greatest news we can receive?

   _____

   What is the greatest news we have to share?

   _____ John 3:16

#-2.   What is the measure of your worth and value, and of each person you meet?

   _____

#-3.   Who are we offending when we look down on one of God's children with haughty eyes?

   _____

   Scripture Proverbs 6:16&17. Matthew 18:10.

#-4.   All things were created by?

   _____

   and for?_____.

   Whom were you created for?

   _____ Scripture Colossians 1:16

#-5. Who can hold all things together including your life, your family, and the life of the Church?

_____ Scripture Colossians 1:17

#-6. How do we make Jesus supreme in His Church, and in our personal lives? First remember the Church is

_____ and we are

_____.

Scripture Colossians 1:16-18.

Secondly we must get into God's

_____,

trust Him with all our _____.

and lean not on our own_____;

and acknowledge Him in all our?

_____ Scripture– Proverbs 3:5-6

#-7. What motivated God's plan of salvation for us?

_____ Scripture John 3:16.

What motivated Jesus to carry out God's plan of salvation and die for us?

_____

_____

_____ Scripture- John 15:13.

#-8.   Jesus died for us that we might be free from?

_____,

and done with _____,

for sin brings _____.

Scripture 1Peter 2:24 & 4:1 & Romans 6:23

#-9.   How did God display His love for us at Calvary?

_____

_____

_____. John 3:16

How did Jesus, Gods Son display His love for the Heavenly Father, and for each of us?

_____

_____. John 15:13

#-10.   Since God values you so much, how much then should you value God?

_____

If God loves you so much, to live for you, and die for you, and live within you, how much then should you love the Lord your God? Are you willing to

_____for Him, and_____

_____for Him too?   Scripture Luke 9:23-24

#-11. After God sent his one and only begotten Son, His gift of love and grace to you, what must you do to accept and receive Gods gift of love?

_____

and be_____

in the name of Jesus Christ. Scripture Acts 2:37-38

#-12. What do we receive when we accept Jesus, Gods gifts of love and grace?

The gift of the_____,

life more_____

eternal_____,

God's gift of_____,

complete_____

and_____.

Scripture acts 2:38-39 John 10:10 17:26 14:27 & Romans 5:5

Following, are a few of the great promises, of what God's love brings to our lives, when the great gift of God's love has been poured into our hearts by the Holy Spirit.

Jesus said: "if anyone loves me, he will keep my word; and my Father will love him, and we will come to him and make our abode with him." John 14:23

"If anyone acknowledges that Jesus is the Son of God, God lives in him and he is in God. And so we know and rely on the love God has for us." 1 John 4:16

"How great is the love the Father has lavished on us, that we should be called the children of God." 1 John 3:1

Chapter Two: "Our Love for God"

As we step into the second dimension of God's love, "Our love for God," let us activate and engage our minds in this all important question.

What is the True Purpose of Life?

We are given many functions and purposes in our lives here on earth. But the question is, what is our main purpose? Knofel Staton said: "Be sure to keep the main thing, the main thing." And I would add if we miss the main thing, the main and true purpose of life, we will miss everything!

The Bible describes life as a vapor or a mist. I can look back 60 years and tell you, life is but a short span. Life is given to us in this short probationary period of time here on earth by our Heavenly Father to determine one thing. And that one thing being the main thing, and "true purpose of life" is this: <u>will we choose to have a "true love relationship" with our Heavenly Father, through Jesus Christ our Lord? That is the main purpose of each of our God given lives here on earth</u>. Each one of us is given a short probationary period here on earth to determine whether we will voluntarily choose of our own free will to have a "True Love Relationship" with our Heavenly Father, by uniting our spirits with His through Jesus, God's Son. A true love relationship with our Heavenly Father is the main purpose our lives were created and designed. If we fail in the main purpose for which we were designed, we will lose everything!

Have you ever wondered why God created us? The triune God head existed from eternity without us, and we are a lot of trouble. Only through the revelation of God's own word lays the answer to this question. **"God is love. Whoever lives in love lives in God, and God in them. In this way love is made complete."**(1John 4:16&17). God's spirit of love completes us. And we are designed and created to complete God's love. <u>To complete the love of God is our true purpose and given destiny.</u>

I believe that God created us in His very own image that through us, He might attain the greatest achievement and reward of all His creation, "True Love Relationships." And that too is our greatest achievement and reward in life, to have "True Love Relationships" with our Heavenly Father, and His children, which is provided for us through the Spirit of God's love in Christ Jesus, our Lord. Life is all about relationships. Our relationship with Jesus will determine our joy, our peace, and the final judgement of our lives. Our final destiny will be determined by the relationship we chose to have with our Heavenly Father and with His children. Our true purpose in life, is to receive God's love cast upon us within our hearts, and return God's love to Him. Having seen and received the immeasurable dimension of "God's love for us," how then are we to use God's gift of love to fulfill the second dimension of God's love, "our love for God?"

CHAPTER TWO: "OUR LOVE FOR GOD"

GOD SHOWS US THE WAY TO EXPRESS "OUR LOVE FOR GOD," THROUGH JESUS!

"And we know that in all things God works for the good of those who love Him, who have been called according to His purpose. For those God foreknew, He also predestined to <u>be conformed to the likeness of His Son,</u> that He might be the firstborn among many brothers. (Roman's 8: 28 & 29.) "But if anyone obeys His word, God's love is truly made complete in him: Whoever claims to live in Him must walk as Jesus did." (1 John 2: 5 & 6.)

Jesus is the way to knowing and loving God! Our Heavenly Father not only sent Jesus to die for us and pay the penalty of our sins, He also sent Jesus to live for us, to show us the way to being children of the Heavenly King. If we have died to Jesus, and are born in His spirit, then we must walk as Jesus walked, presenting our bodies as living sacrifices, holy and pleasing to God. For this was the walk of Jesus, and walking the walk of Jesus is our true act of spiritual worship in expressing "our love for God."

Let us look in on the life of Jesus, our example for knowing and loving God. We find Him at the age of twelve as His parents did in the temple courts. Let us listen in. **"After three days they found Him in the temple courts, sitting among the teachers, listening to them and asking them questions. Everyone who heard Him was amazed at His understanding and His answers.**

When His parents saw Him, they were astonished. His mother said to Him, "Son, why have You treated us like this? Your father and I have been anxiously searching for You."

"Why were you searching for Me?" He asked. "Didn't you know I had to be in My Father's house?" But they did not understand what He was saying to them. Then He went down to Nazareth with them and was obedient to them. But His mother treasured all these things in her heart. And Jesus grew in wisdom and stature, and in favor with God and men." (Luke 2: 46-52.)

What can we learn from this segment of Jesus' life on how to walk as Jesus walked, and how to express "our love for God?"

- Jesus was listening to the teachings of God and asking questions. We first learn that Jesus was a good listener. We have many types of speech classes throughout our school system to teach us how to express ourselves. But I don't know of any listening classes to teach us how to be good listeners. Good listening is a prerequisite for proper speaking and discernment. When we listen to God's word with our minds and hearts, and then in our love of God ask questions to know of Him better, we express "our love for God."

- They were amazed at Jesus understanding. Jesus had great understanding, because Jesus had great listening skills, that leads to great discernment. When we give ourselves to the listening and discernment of God's word, and allow our Lord's words to direct our lives, we express "our love for God."

Chapter Two: "Our Love For God"

- Jesus said: "Didn't you know I had to be in my Father's house?" "Our love for God," is being where we know God expects us to be. I'm glad when I hear the Church bells ring, and the Church doors are opened. I'm glad to be in the presence of the Spirit of the Lord, and receive His promise. **"For where two or three have gathered in My name, I am there in their midst."** (Matthew 18:20.) I'm glad to be in the household of God, for the Church is the highest institution of learning; only the Church of God teaches the many facets of God's wisdom, which include God's plan of salvation and the unfathomable riches of Christ. Only through the Church of God is the manifold wisdom of God being displayed. **"His intent was that now, through the Church, the manifold wisdom of God should be made known."** (Ephesians 3:10.) I am glad to be in the Lord's Church, for I want to fulfill my Lord's desire to encourage His people and be encouraged. **"And let us consider how we may spur one another on toward love and good deeds. Let us not give up meeting together, as some are in the habit of doing, but let us encourage one another– and all the more as you see the Day approaching."** (Hebrews 10:24 & 25.)

When we assemble ourselves together in the household of God, we express "our love for God." When we encourage the members of His Body, in continuing their walk of love and service to the Lord, we express "our love for God." We express our love to the hurting when we listen with sincere and caring hearts. Yes! We express our love for God, when we express love for our brothers and sisters in Christ.

- How can we know we have found the Lord's church? Jesus said: **"A new command I give you that you love one another, even as I have loved you, that you also love one another. By this all men will know you are My disciples if you have love for one another."** (John 13:34 & 35.) You have found the Lord's Body (the Church) when you see and feel the Spirit of the Lord's love, and you are glad you came, and they know your name, where the Lord's word and teachings are not white washed, but taught in love and truth. A place that allows and encourages you to serve in the highest vocation given unto man, serving in our Lord's kingdom. When we serve our Lord and His Kingdom, we express "our love for God."

- The result of Jesus life style and custom, **"Jesus grew in wisdom and stature, and in favor with God and men."** And so will we, when we walk as Jesus walked. When we learn to walk as Jesus walked, carrying out His Father's will in all we say and do we are expressing "our love for God."

CHAPTER TWO: "OUR LOVE FOR GOD"

"OUR LOVE FOR GOD" IS TO WALK THE WALK OF JESUS!

Walking with Jesus gives proper direction in our lives, and frees our spirits. Jesus said: **"Come to Me, all you who are weary and burdened, and I will give you rest. Take My yoke upon you and learn from Me, for I am gentle and humble in heart, and you will find rest for your souls. For My yoke is easy and My burden is light."** (Matthew 11:28-30.) From the preceding words of our Lord, what can we learn to help us in our spiritual quest to walk as Jesus walked? Following are a few of my thoughts. I'm sure as you read them and dwell on the words of Jesus, you will be able to add to them.

- Jesus not only freed us from our sins, He also lightens our burdens when we walk with Him. And we will not grow weary in our walk with Jesus. Jesus enlightens our way as we learn to walk in His gentle and humble way.

- Whom would you prefer to walk with or work with, someone who is harsh and proud, or someone who is gentle and humble? We don't always have a choice of whom we work with, but we do have the choice of daily walking with Jesus.

- I've been down the road of harshness and pride, with others and with myself. And the road of pride is a hard road that burdens you, and those around you; one has to walk carefully around the proud, for they are very touchy and easily provoked.

- I choose to walk the road of gentleness and humbleness, and that road calls for walking with Jesus. Jesus is the epitome of the gentleness and humbleness that I desire in myself and with whom I walk, for they are easy to be around, and its easier living with yourself when pride doesn't trip you up and embarrass you. For being yoked to Jesus is easy and the burden is light. Walking with Jesus in His gentle and humble way, and learning from Him, expresses "our love for God."

In our walk with Jesus and conforming to His likeness, Jesus teaches us the proper manner in praying to our Heavenly Father. The power of prayer lies in proper praying.

CHAPTER TWO: "OUR LOVE FOR GOD"

JESUS TEACHES US TO PRAY!

Jesus said: this then, is how you should pray:

> **"Our Father in heaven,**
> **Hallowed be your name,**
> **Your kingdom come,**
> **Your will be done**
> **On earth as it is in heaven.**
> **Give us today our daily bread.**
> **Forgive us our debts,**
> **As we also have forgiven our**
> **Debtors.**
> **And lead us not into temptation,**
> **but deliver us from the evil one."**
> (Matthew 6:9-13)

- I always stand amazed in the presence of Jesus' teachings. Jesus' model prayer that He gave for us to pray daily unto our Heavenly Father is clear and concise, and yet it covers our every need.

- <u>First</u>-- our prayer is to begin with praise, **"Our Father in heaven hallowed be your name."** From this point each of our prayers will vary in our personal acknowledgment of our Father, acknowledging Him in our plans for the new day, and asking for His divine intervention and guidance. And then we need to give our personal praise and thanksgiving for the past and present blessings our Father has bestowed upon us.

- Secondly-- we pray for the advancement of our Father's Kingdom, and for His will to be done on earth as it is in heaven. **"Your Kingdom come, and Your will be done, on earth as it is in heaven."** Again, this part of our prayer can be expanded upon due to the insights and position of each individual. It's a time we can ask God's will to be done through us, and that He open doors of opportunity to advance His Kingdom. Also, it is a time we can call upon the Lord for spiritual healing, for ourselves, and others we know that are in need. And pray that our Lord's perfect and pleasing will be done in our lives.

- Thirdly—the Lord's prayer calls for us to pray daily for our physical needs. **"Give us today our daily bread."** And here again each person may call upon our Heavenly Father for their own personal needs, and the needs of others they know. Maybe we or someone we know needs' physical healing or the need might be work, food or clothing. Then we need to ask the Lord to show us the way in helping to meet those needs. And ask the Lord's help in meeting the unseen needs that our Lord sees. In all things ask for the Lord's divine intervention and that His will be done. Pray for God's wisdom and discernment in meeting our physical needs, and for helping in the needs of those He sends our way.

- Fourth—the Lord's prayer calls for us to pray for forgiveness. **"Forgive us our debts, <u>as</u> we also have forgiven our debtors."** In the preceding directions of our Lord, we are assured that the divine procedure, in the matter of forgiveness, that our forgiveness from the Father, will be exactly in the order that we have forgiven others their trespasses. As a matter of fact, in following our Lord's teaching, we pray for our sins to be forgiven from the Father in the very same manner we have forgiven one another. Our Lord in His love for us does this in our best interest, for to be spiritually free we must forgive others in the same manner that we want forgiveness from the Father. One is never free who holds animosities in their heart; the design of our Heavenly Father's forgiveness sets our spirits free. Forgiveness is truly divine, for it proceeds from God, setting our spirits free from guilt and animosity.

- <u>Lastly</u>–our Lord's prayer calls for us to petition our Father for His divine guidance and protection. **"And lead us not into temptation, but deliver us from the evil one."** The protection of our Lord comes to us through carrying our Lord's written directives in our hearts and minds, and by listening to the gift of God's Spirit placed in our hearts, and then simply by God's own divine intervening power our Father protects us. Whenever our life rests in the mighty Hand of our Lord, we can then walk in the assurance that God's mighty power is surrounding us, and His protective hand will hold us up.

Check out our Lord's model prayer and see if it doesn't cover our every need. What a great privilege we have been given through Jesus to petition our Heavenly Father with our needs, and what a great peace of mind we are given, when we carry our every need to our Heavenly Father, Almighty God, Creator, and sustaining power over all, and the lover of our souls. Through Jesus we express our ways, our prayers, and "our love for God."

"Our love for God" intertwines within our relationships with others.

"When the Son of Man comes in His glory, and all the angels with Him, He will sit on His throne in heavenly glory. All the nations will gather before Him, and He will separate the people one from another as a shepherd separates the sheep from the goats. He will put the sheep on His right and the goats on His left.

Then the king will say to those on His right, come you who are blessed by My Father; take your inheritance, the Kingdom prepared for you since the creation of the world. For I was hungry and you gave me something to eat, I was thirsty and you gave Me something to drink, I was a stranger and you invited Me in, I needed clothes and you clothed Me, I was sick and you looked after Me, I was in prison and you came to visit Me.

Then the righteous will answer Him, Lord, when did we see You hungry and feed You, or thirsty and give You something to drink? When did we see You a stranger and invite You in, or needing clothes and clothed You? When did we see You sick or in prison and go to visit You?

The King will reply, I tell you the truth, whatever you did for one of the least of these brothers of mine, you did for Me.

Then He will say to those on His left, 'Depart from Me, you who are cursed, into the eternal fire prepared for the

devil and his angels. For I was hungry and you gave Me nothing to eat, I was thirsty and you gave Me nothing to drink, I was a stranger and you did not invite Me in, I needed clothes and you did not clothe Me, I was sick and in prison and you did not look after Me;

They will also answer; 'Lord, when did we see you hungry or thirsty or a stranger or needing clothes or sick or in prison, and did not help You?

He will reply, I tell you the truth, whatever you did not do for one of the least of these, you did not do for Me;

Then they will go away to eternal punishment, but the righteous to eternal life."

(Matthew 25:31-46)

Jesus' words and parables are divine spiritual truths, given for our spirits to feed upon, and grow into the likeness and knowledge of our Lord. Let us list and digest the words of Jesus for our spiritual growth, and "our love for God."

- Our relationship with Jesus' brothers and sisters, and our treatment of them reflects on Jesus.

- Jesus feels the joy and pain of each of us, and He knows the source of our joy and pain.

- Those blessed by the Heavenly Father, are those who minister to the needs of others.

- The service of the righteous was out of love for the one in needs, not to win favor for their selves from the Lord.

- Love seeks the best interest of others without seeking the applause of man or God for their work.

- True members of the Lord's spiritual body, serves the needs of others in love and compassion just as the Lord's physical body served while here on earth.

- Only the Lord adds body members to His church, and only the Lord determines who inherits the riches of His kingdom.

- Many self-proclaimed body members who failed to express God's love in serving the needs of others will hear these horrifying words of the Lord: **"depart from me, you who are cursed, into the eternal fire prepared for the devil and his angels."**

- Our relationship with our Lord, and our destiny, is intertwined in our relationship with others.

Jesus' parable speaks volumes of how we are to express "Our love for God." When we express our love to others through acts of kindness, we are also expressing "our love for God!"

The greatest achievement and reward in this short probationary period of God given life, is to receive God's love cast upon us into open hearts, and then return God's gift of love, unto our Heavenly Father. A true love relationship with our Heavenly Father, and Children of the Heavenly King, is life's greatest achievement and reward. Life without relationships would be like hitting a hole in one! But we couldn't share it with anyone. Life without "true love relationships" is like receiving the greatest news you ever received, or making the greatest accomplishment in your life, but you have no one to share it with. But, God, in His infinite wisdom, created and designed our lives for interdependence, not for self dependence. We are designed with a will to share our good news and joy, as well as our bad news and hurts, with other free will agents of God's creation equipped with loving and caring hearts, that can feel our joy and pain.

The proper functioning for our lives is based on a proper relationship with our Lord and Heavenly Father, and with God's children. These proper relationships are forerunners for producing a good relationship within ourselves. One can never be right within their self until they are right with God. And being right with God demands a "true love relationship" with our Heavenly Father, produced through the oneness of spirit with our Lord. Life is all about relationships, "true love relationships" will complete our lives, and secure for us, a blissful destiny! "True love relationships" can only be attained and maintained through God's love. The ways we return God's love, are to attain, cherish, nourish, and maintain a "true love relationship" with our Heavenly Father, and God's children, through being one in the Spirit of Jesus our Lord.

"TRUE LOVE RELATIONSHIPS"

"True love relationships" are not measured by blood lines, marriage certificates, memberships, nor time gone by.

"True love relationships" are measured by receiving
and giving hearts of God's Spirit and love,
One to another;

Time can't touch God, nor take away His eternal Spirit and love, which shall seal and bond our spirits together forever.

Lasting and meaningful relationships are measured by God's gift of love, given and received one to another.

THREE IMPORTANT TRUTHS THAT MUST EXIST IN A "TRUE LOVE RELATIONSHIP."

#-1---LOVE MUST BE VOLUNTARY!

God, in seeking the greatest and most desired achievement of His creation, which I believe were "true love relationships" that will last through eternity, created man and woman in His image, with the capabilities of receiving and returning His love. In order to achieve His goal God created men and women to be free will beings, because love by it's very nature must be voluntary. If we are really to love God, men and women must be able to choose of their own free will to love God in response to God's love for them. Therefore, if we are given the right to make right moral choices, we must necessarily be given the right to make wrong moral choices.

A major function in being a free will agent which self imposes the direction of our lives, is that God created within our hearts and minds, a door that only we can open and close to whomever and whatever we choose. God designed this free will mechanism within our hearts and minds, because He wants us to voluntarily choose to receive and return His love. For an involuntary love is a contradiction in terms and there can be no such thing.

Our hearts and minds are filled with what we choose to open them to. Therefore, it is of the utmost importance that we know that whatever we choose to fill our hearts and minds with, that is what will overflow from us in words and deeds. Good stuff in, good stuff out, bad stuff in, bad stuff out. The words we speak and the actions we take are mere reflections of what lies within our hearts and minds. We are the door keepers of our hearts. The choice is ours to whom and what we will open our hearts and minds. Only hearts that voluntarily open their heart doors to God, to be filled with His love, will achieve the blessings of God's love. The number one blessing of God's love is a "true love relationship" with Jesus our Lord, and our Heavenly Father, and His children, for today and throughout eternity.

God has voluntarily opened the door of His heart to each of us through Jesus. The doorway to God's love is open when we voluntarily choose to open the door of our heart to Jesus, God's gift of love. "True love relationships" consist of voluntary love of both parties. To complete the purpose of our life, we must voluntarily open our hearts to the inflow and outflow of God's love.

#-2—Love must be reciprocal!

For the existence of a "true love relationship" God's love must be reciprocal. When we give our love, it must be returned, and when we receive the love of another, we must return their love, for a "true love relationship" to exist.

For a "true love relationship" to begin and exist one party must open their heart to the other party. When we chose to do this, we are running a risk in order to achieve life's greatest reward, a "true love relationship." The Heavenly Father is our great example of running a risk for "true love relationships." God opened His heart and soul to you and me when He sent to us His one and only begotten Son. God, in sending us His Son, was saying this is who I Am! In My Son is My love and grace for you. If we choose to open our hearts and receive God's Spirit of love through God's Son we are then filled with His Spirit of love, and united as one, with our Heavenly Father in a "true love relationship," as His Children. Our Heavenly Father surely knew He ran the risk of having His love rejected, but thought it worth the risk to attain life's greatest achievement, "true love relationships."

Christians must be as Christ, they must be transparent, opening their hearts and giving their love from God to those they meet. All should know who you are, by their description of you. All mysterious and hidden corners of our hearts should be cleansed and filled with the transparency of Christ Spirit. Jesus Christ the Bright and Morning Star, shines the beams of His Spirit

Chapter Two: "Our Love For God"

of love, out through us, into a darkened world. At times will our projected love, receive rejection as our Lord's did? Yes! But we must run that risk in order to attain and receive life's greatest reward, "true love relationships" with Jesus our Lord, the Heavenly Father, and His children. Also we will receive the reward and joy of seeing God's lost children led to Christ our Savior, and then seeing unproductive lives becoming productive, broken hearts, and broken homes, mended and healed by the Word and Spirit of our Lord. The joy of the Lord abounds within us, when we see our friends and loved ones filled with the Love and Joy of Christ. With the spirit of Christ's love and joy dwelling in us does this mean we should never feel nor express sadness and anger? Jesus was described by Isaiah as a man of sorrow! Jesus wept over Jerusalem, for God's children rejected His love and grace. When we see our children refusing to walk in God's love and grace, we must weep. We can't walk in this world without a heartfelt sadness for the lost, and for the pain sin brings. Jesus used a whip and turned over the money changer's tables driving them out of His Father's temple for the misuse of His Father's house, His house of prayer. There are times when Christians need to pick up the whip of Jesus, and in His righteous anger, lash out at the sin against God.

While a "true love relationship" with our Lord and Heavenly Father, and His children are life's greatest reward and achievement, unrequited love is life's greatest tragedy! Unrequited love is for one to open their heart to another, giving them their love, and they do not return their love. For the proper functioning of our lives, and the life of a church body, God's love must be reciprocal.

They say a picture is worth a thousand words. There are some pictures in my mind of unrequited love, which I can project to you. One is seeing a bumper sticker on a truck stating: "I love my truck." What a sad love affair, you may love your truck, but your truck doesn't love you! Another picture comes from an old song "Delta Dawn" one of the lyric's states: "Delta Dawn what's that flower you have on, could it be a faded rose from days gone by?"

I see her with a faded flower upon her blouse, covering a fainted heart, as she stands on a street corner waiting for the love of her heart, that never returns. And another picture also remains in my mind, a picture of four church ladies. They came up out of the church basement from their quilting party one day to have their picture taken on the church steps, for having it placed in the local newspaper advertizing for church members, for the ladies feared their church was going to close. Only God's reciprocal love through Christ, keeps hearts vibrantly alive in serving our Lord's great commission. A love for the Lord, and a love for the lost, are what keeps the doors of His Church open.

If these pictures I have projected to you are not convincing enough that life's greatest tragedy is unrequited love, let me give you another snapshot that should explode with technique color and cinema scope within your heart and mind. I see people crying out, **"Lord! Lord!"**(Matthew 7:22) when Christ returns again, and then they hear these horrifying words from our Lord; **"Depart from Me, into the fire prepared for the devil and his angels, I never knew you!"**(Matthew 7:23 & 25:41). There will be no greater tragedy to mankind, than to those who reject God's love. This should be an everlasting picture and reminder in our hearts and minds, that our mission from the Lord is to share His love and good news, making disciples of those who come into our lives. Yes, God's unrequited love is life's greatest tragedy! But God's reciprocal love through Christ is life's greatest blessing! To those who choose to allow God's love to flow into their hearts, and then choose to allow God's love to flow through them vertically back to God, and horizontally out to the objects of God's love, they will hear the most rewarding words of their life, from their Lord: **"Well done, good and faithful servant! You have been faithful with a few things; I will put you in charge of many things. Come and share your Master's joy."**(Matthew 25:21). To complete the purpose of our lives, God's love must be reciprocal, and love must be based on trust.

Chapter Two: "Our Love For God"

#-3—Love Must be Based on Trust!

A "true love relationship" with our Lord and Heavenly Father and His children must be based on trust. We can trust God's word and promises to be true and upheld by God. But, can the Lord trust us to obey and uphold His teaching and commandments? Yes! I believe He can, when we open our hearts to the enabling power of God's Spirit dwelling in us. And our faith in God's teachings and commands, will grow all the more when we see how the teachings of Jesus will enlighten and empower us along our pathway of life. Will we stumble? I believe we all will occasionally, but hopefully not often as we grow in Christ. But when we do stumble, Christ our Lord through His word and through His divine intervention, and through His brothers and sisters will be there to pick us up. We should always be there for our Lord to pick up a brother or sister when they fall. But we may always be assured our Lord will be there when we fall to pick us up, and dust us off, and send us on His way, when we reach up to Him in our needs, and in faith. The main thing we must do is remain faithful to being in the Word, and the fellowship of the Saints of God.

Trust must be exercised and maintained in any relationship, for broken trust leads to broken hearts and broken relationships. We must learn to place our trust in people for they will usually try to measure up to the trust and confidence we place in them. And always trust in the Lord with all our heart, for God always measures up to our trust. No "true love relationship" can exist without trust being applied from both parties. God's Holy Scripture gives these directives for our lives, along with a great promise that will lead us to a great and productive life. We must learn to apply these words in our personal life and the life of the Church. **"Trust in the Lord with all your heart and lean not on your own understanding; in all your ways acknowledge Him, and He will make your paths straight."** (Proverbs 3:5&6) How are we to do this in our personal lives and in the life of the Church Body? <u>Before making every decision, we must acknowledge our Lord in believing prayer, then follow His directives in carrying out our decisions. God's directives come to us through His written word, and through the voice of His Holy Spirit living in our hearts.</u> For our hearts to be attuned to our Lord's will, our hearts and minds must always be in communication with our Lord. Like the cell phone I see attached to some folk's ear, we must keep the spirit of our Lord attached to our hearts and minds, fully trusting in His voice to direct our lives, as we sacrifice our will and life, into the will and life of Christ.

CHAPTER TWO: "OUR LOVE FOR GOD"

THROUGH SACRIFICE WE EXPRESS "OUR LOVE FOR GOD."

A "true love relationship" can never be attained between two people through compromise but rather through the sacrifice of their selves into one spirit. A "true love relationship" between us and our Heavenly Father, and between one another, will only exist when we individually sacrifice ourselves into the spirit of Jesus. Jesus said: **" I am the way and the truth and the life. No one comes to the Father except through me."** (John 14:6.) The spirit of Jesus connects us to the spirit of the Heavenly Father, and to one another when we sacrifice ourselves into the way of the Lord. It is the old triangle story we learned in Vacation Bible School.

The closer we draw into the Spirit of Jesus the closer we draw to one another. When we become one in the Spirit of Christ, we become one in the Spirit of our Heavenly Father, and those in

Christ. This sacrifice comes by full submission and trusting in the Lord with our lives.

After the Church service one Sunday morning, a young boy named Curtis came up to me and asked if he could be baptized. Baptism is a public statement, and an outward act of a full submission of what you are feeling in your heart for Jesus. Christian baptism represents putting to death your old self, and then being born anew in Christ. We accomplish this public statement and plea to God, by having our entire body buried into a watery grave, and dying to Christ Jesus, then breaking up through the water as a babe breaks through the water of their mother's womb to be born anew. And then as babes in Christ, having our sins washed away, we begin to walk in a newness of life in Christ Jesus, and having Jesus walking with us through the promised gift of His Holy Spirit, living in us and for us.

Expressing Curtis' desire to be baptized into Jesus to a couple of the Church elders, they told me I probably should talk to Curtis, to make sure he understood what Christian baptism entails. I sat down with Curtis with well-prepared information on Christian baptism. My first question was, "Curtis why do you want to be baptized?" Curtis replied with his young hand patting his heart, "Jim, I feel it right here in my heart!" I closed my Bible and went back to the elders and told them Curtis is ready to be baptized. There are two ministries that occur in presenting the gospel message of Jesus. My ministry, the ministry of the living word, was to preach the gospel message of Jesus in truth and love, with clarity. There is a second ministry that occurs at the same time, the ministry of the Holy Spirit. The first ministry of the Holy Spirit is to convict our hearts of sin, and a desire to follow Jesus. Curtis had heard of Jesus' love for him, and then he had a heartfelt desire to love and follow Jesus. We teach and preach the gospel message, but only God can read and convict a heart. Only Christ through the working of the Holy Spirit adds a member to His Body, the Church. Who am I to ever interfere with the ministry of the Holy Spirit? Curtis' wish was granted; he was baptized into Jesus, and was able to return the love he felt in his heart for Jesus, by doing what the Lord asks us to do.

"OUR LOVE FOR GOD" IS FOLLOWING GOD'S COMMANDMENTS!

How do we return God's love? We return God's love by the way He directs us. God's Holy Word say's, **"This is love for God: to obey His commandments. And His commandments are not burdensome."** (1 John 5:3). Indeed our Heavenly Father's commandments are not burdensome. They are a blessing to our lives and to those around us. God's love for us motivated His plan of salvation for us. And it is our love for God that motivates us to do what He asks us to do. And what He asks us to do really is not so difficult at all. Following God's commandments of love is good for our lives, the lives around us, and the life of His Church. Our loving Heavenly Father's love seeks what is best for us.

For a "true love relationship" with our Lord, can He trust us to return His love by following His commandments? We especially should know and follow our Lord's first and greatest commandment. I am amazed at the number of Christians I have encountered over the years who gave their life to Christ in Christian baptism, which is a public statement of making Jesus, lord of their lives, cannot tell me what the first and greatest command is, that their Lord gave them to follow. If Jesus is really Lord of our life, and the Lord of our life told us to pick cotton what should our response be? Give me a cotton bag, and show me the field, Lord Jesus!

Chapter Two: "Our Love For God"

What we need are more first commandment Churches. If we are not a first commandment disciples, and the Church is not a first commandment Church body, we are not living members of the body of Christ. The bodies of Christ are members of His body carrying out the will of their Lord, the head of the Church. Why is it so important for us as members of the body of Christ to know and follow our Lord's first and greatest command? First of all, if we know and follow the first and greatest command we will want to know and follow all the rest of our Lord's commands and precepts. The success of our personal lives and the life of the Lord's Church is dependent upon our knowing and following our Lord's first and greatest command.

Life is dependent upon our knowing and following our Lord's commands. One of the first things our military soldiers learn in basic training is their general orders and chain of commands. And they don't leave basic training to serve their country until they have memorized them. To make sure each military soldier knows the chain of commands and general orders before they move on to serve their country, they are required to repeat them to their drill sergeant while they are in your face, with their nose pressing against your nose, just to make sure nothing intimidates you from knowing and carrying out what you are commanded to do. And they are just hoping you might just miss one of them. Let's just say you will never, ever want to miss knowing your commands again.

A great military protects its country and conquers its foes by marching in unison to their orders and commands. Can you imagine giving each military personnel a uniform and weapon and they're not willing to know and carry out the commands of their commander and chief? Life as we know it would become a jungle of caustic events.

Christian soldiers what did our Commander and Chief, our Lord and Savior, tell us to pray for daily right after giving thanks and praise unto our Heavenly Father? The advancement of God's

Kingdom! **"Your Kingdom come your will be done on earth as it is in heaven."**(Matthew 6:10) The earth is being overcome by religious factions of hate. We have a much greater need than sending another 100,000 military troops into other nations, we need to send and support 100,000 missionaries teaching the Love of God! As we are called by our Lord to pray daily for the advancement of God's Kingdom throughout the earth, we must also support the advancement of God's Kingdom with our giving and service. For there is nothing more important and urgent in our lives here on earth than carrying out our Lord's Great Commission. **"Therefore go and make disciples of all nations, baptizing them in the name of the Father and of the Son and of the Holy Spirit."**(Matthew 28:19) Satan and his forces are marching against the army of God. Christian soldiers must arise to the battle call of our Commander and Chief to advance the Word and Spirit of our Lord unto all nations. The world must receive the Spirit of God's love to overcome the destructive hate of Satan and his evil forces. Rise up Christian soldiers in the Love of our mighty God in carrying out our mission here on earth, **"Therefore go and make disciples of all nations."**

Christian soldiers of the cross of Jesus, we serve under an infallible Commander and Chief who marches us, and enables us, against the world's greatest foe, which is sin and death! We have been given our Lord's message of reconciliation to carry forth in love and unity, to free those outside of Christ Spirit of unity and love. Loved ones are being deceived by the evil forces of Satan who has them bound in their sins, and they are awaiting the penalty of death! Christian soldiers, the lives of your relatives, friends, and neighbors are dependent upon you carrying out your commission and mission! Do you know the commission and mission the Lord has given His Christian soldiers? Christian soldiers, we cannot move forward in accomplishing the mission of our Lord, the head of the Church body, without knowing and following our Lord's first and greatest command. The fulfillment of our Lord's first and greatest command motivates and energizes us, into carrying out our mission from our Chief and Commander. If Jesus is Lord of our lives, we must place our Lord's first and greatest command in our hearts and minds, and then carry it out every day of our lives. Jesus was asked, "Of all the commandments, which is the most important?" Jesus replied: **"the Lord our God is one Lord; and you shall love the Lord your God with all your heart, and with all your soul, and with all your mind, and with all your strength."**(Mark 12:30.) On another occasion Jesus was asked by an expert in the law; "Teacher, what must I do to inherit eternal life?" Jesus replied to him; **"What is written in the law? "And how do you read it?"** He answered: **"You shall love the Lord your God with all your heart, and with all your soul, and with all your strength, and with all your mind' and, 'love your neighbor as yourself."** Jesus replied: **"You have answered correctly, do this and you will live."**(Luke 10:25-28.).

Christian soldiers must march in unison to the step and drumbeat of God's love. We must carry forth the banner of "God's love for us" by the conquering power of "our love for God" into a world overcome and bound by Satan. We must defeat him and free God's children with our Lord's message of reconciling love. What's at stake in our knowing our Lord's first and greatest command, and carrying it forth with all our mind, with all our heart, with all our soul, and with all our strength? Life and death! The life of our friends and neighbors, and our very own life, is dependent upon our knowing and carrying out our Lord's first and greatest command. God's love is the victor, the conqueror of sin and death! Christian soldiers we have been enlisted through the blood of Jesus to carry forth with all our mind, heart, soul, and strength, the life saving power of God's love, with the aroma of victory before us, let the mighty army of God march onward in the unity of God's love. Clearly, we have been called, to carry forth the love of the Lord our God, with every fiber of our being.

Christian soldiers must put on the armor of battle every day, and give all their allegiance to carrying out our Lord's will and commands. We must give all "our love for God" in loving service to King Jesus.

<u>With all our heart!</u> Means with all our affection we are to adore, idolize, and worship, the Lord our God. We are to open our hearts to God, allowing Him through the Holy Spirit to fill our hearts with His love. We are to serve our Lord's dear cause with hearts overflowing with His Love.

<u>With All Our Soul!</u> With all our life we are to love and serve our God, when we arise, in our walk in life, in our family, in our work place, in His Church, and when we lie down, we are to love and serve the Lord our God. Every facet of our life is to give and show "our love for God." In music soul means with feeling, our lives must become marching symphonies of God's love flowing from us.

<u>With All Our Mind!</u> We are to love and serve our Lord our God with all our intellect. Wisdom comes from God. Let us call upon Him in the early morning to activate our minds in the way of loving and serving our Lord. We also must read and study our Lords' instructions, precepts, and teachings, and then carry them out in our lives by the enabling power of the Holy Spirit. We must speak our mind to the Lord in reverent prayer, aligning our mind set to the mind set of our Lord.

<u>With All Our Strength!</u> We are to give our energy to the missions and causes of our Lord, by carrying out our Lord's commands, His teachings, and His precepts. **"Therefore, I urge you, brothers in view of God's mercy, to offer your bodies as living sacrifices, holy and pleasing to God—this is your spiritual act of worship"** (Romans' 12:1.) We are to be living sacrifices carrying out "our love for God." There are an amazing number of people carrying

Chapter Two: "Our Love For God"

the name of Christ, Christian, and claiming Jesus as Lord of their lives, that cannot tell you what their Lord's first and greatest command is that He gave them to carry out.

I went to barber college right after high school. My intent was to gain a trade and later get a college degree. Fifteen years later I received a two-year college degree, sometimes, our plans get derailed. I married my beautiful wife Sandra, and six months later I was drafted into the army. According to the draft letter I was drafted by my good friends and neighbors, none of their names were listed, probably just as well. Sandra and I had our first child before I was shipped out to Germany. Cindy was six weeks old when I left and was a year and half old when I returned. Young people are fortunate they no longer have to deal with a draft system that keeps your life on hold. Upon my return I opened and operated a barber shop. I also became a Christian at age twenty seven. Being a young devout Christian, it was my habit to never miss Church services. I was glad when the Church bells rang and the Church doors were opened. I studied my bible, and listened to religious services on the radio. One day I was giving one of my customer's who attended a non instrumentalist Church a haircut. Having heard his minister give a message on the radio, I decided to initiate some conversation by telling Ron I had heard his minister on the radio, and that I thought he was doing a good job, good P. R. for business you know. What wasn't good for business I went ahead and said, "I don't know why though he would waste air time telling why you don't have a piano in your Church." Ron would later return to give me verse and scripture, why there should be no musical instruments in the Church. And I would counter with scriptures that I believed defended musical instruments in worship service. A few days later Ron brought his minister to the shop. The debate continued on, until it became very spiritually tiring for me, and I began praying to the Lord about the particular matter.

A few weeks later as I was cutting Ron's hair one day, during the course of our conversation I seemed to detect that Ron did not know our Lord's first and greatest command. I walked around to the front of the chair and asked Ron if he knew the Lord's first and greatest command. After giving a couple of futile attempts at giving the answer, Ron admitted he did not know. I asked Ron how long he had been attending church there. He told me two years. I said to him: "Ron in two years the Church has taught you verse and scripture why there should be no musical instrument in the Church, but they have not taught you your Lord's first and greatest command. Do you see now why the church has greater things to speak about and teach, than whether or not the Church should have musical instruments?" And then I asked Ron if he would bring his preacher in to see me again. I believed we had something more important to discuss. Ron nor his preacher ever returned. I believe Corporate religion is derailing the mission of Christ through their man-made doctrines and priorities.

There is an old story which gives emphasis to the previous story and statement. A congregation got into a dispute over the use of musical instruments in the Church. Finally they split over the disputed issue and each had its own Church building. One day the non instrumentalist slipped over to the instrumental groups Church and hid their piano. A fuss started up again between the two groups, one group demanding to know where they had placed their piano, and the other group refusing to tell. The prank and fuss between the two groups continued on for several months until one day the instrumental group found their piano. Do you know where they found it? They found it in the baptistry! Does this sound like a little kid's story? Sometimes when Christians lose their priorities and stop fulfilling their Lord's commands and commissions they act like children, and not like soldiers of the Heavenly King carrying out their Lord's Great Commission.

We probably all have a story we could share of the Church, being led away from the mission and designed purpose of the

Church, which we have received from Jesus our Lord, the head of the Church. When Christians clash and divide over trivial opinions Christianity loses. Our love for God, and our love for each other must be far greater than our differences. We must allow each other freedom of opinions. But we must never allow our differences to separate us from worshiping and working together in serving our Lord's will in the spirit of His love. The Christian's witness must always reflect to the world love for God, and love for each other. We successfully meet our Lord's designed purpose for our life, and the life of the Church Body, when we totally yield ourselves unto the Lord and His teaching. We are then consumed by the enabling power of the Holy Spirit, which overcomes the spirit of darkness.

THE CAUSE OF DIVISIONS IN THE CHURCH.

The causes of divisions in the Church body are caused by some elected Church leaders who are not in the Spirit of God's Love. It is my hope and prayer that leaders of the Lord's Church bodies will learn to align themselves with the love, patience, and kindness of our great Shepherd. When those who take upon leadership roles in the body of Christ fully submit their lives to Christ, they will lead the Lord's Church bodies into the unity our Lord prayed for in John chapter seventeen. The Spirit of the Lord's love is the great uniting force that overcomes our differences of personalities and non scriptural opinions. I also hope and pray that the Church bodies of Christ will learn to follow our Lord's instructions in selecting leaders full of the Spirit and wisdom of God. When a Church body fails in praying for divine intervention from the Lord, and fails to follow the written instructions of God's Word in their selection of Church leaders, then Satan wins. When we step out of our Lord's instructions, and His Spirit of Love and Wisdom, then the Church body ends up with Church leaders as described in Jude nineteen. **"These are the men who divide you, who follow mere natural instincts and do not have the Spirit."** Divisions are brought about by worldly Church leaders devoid of the Spirit.

We as individual Church members of the body of Christ must ever strive together, to bring about and keep the unity in the Body of Christ. The answer for our learning to live in love and unity, in the Body of Christ, lies in learning how to fully submit our lives into Christ. For Christ is not divided, Christ's Spirit directs us, and unites us, in love and unity. Let us each all together, and always, pray the prayer that our Lord prayed for us. **"That all of them may be one, Father, just as you are in me and I am in you. May they also be one in us that the world may believe that you have sent me."** (John 17:21.) If we are to be effective witnesses for our Lord, then our witness must be a witness of God's Spirit of Love, living within us, that promotes unity of our spirits in the Spirit of Christ. Let us listen to the final words of our Lord's prayer for us. **"I have made you known to them, and will continue to make you known in order that the love you have for me may be in them and that I myself may be in them."** (John 17:26.) May it be our ever lasting desire to be the completion of our Lord's prayer. May our witness to the world and in the Lord's Church ever be of one living in and promoting the Spirit of Love and Unity of our Lord and Heavenly Father. As we look again at Jesus words of prayer, we see in order to fulfill our Lord's prayer we must become the temple that Christ built and lives in, where the Holy Spirit witnesses the Lord's love and unity of the Heavenly Father through us.

CHAPTER TWO: "OUR LOVE FOR GOD"

THE IMPORTANCE OF KNOWING AND FOLLOWING THE COMMANDMENTS OF JESUS.

Do you believe it is important to memorize our Lord's commandments, to have knowledge of His commandments, and to apply them in our lives? For the answer of truth, let us listen in, to our Teacher, and the Teacher of His Church, whom we are messengers of His teaching.

And a lawyer stood up and put Him to the test, saying, "Teacher what shall I do to inherit eternal life?"

And He said to him, "What is written in the law? How does it read to you?"

And he answered, "You shall love the Lord your God with all your heart, and with all your soul, and with all your strength, and with all your mind; and your neighbor as yourself."

And He said to him, "you have answered correctly; DO THIS AND YOU WILL LIVE." (LUKE 10:26-28)

The man asked Jesus, "What must we do to inherit eternal life? Jesus replies to his question with two questions, **"What is written in the law?"** and **"how do you read it?"** We need to note at this point that Jesus did not ask the man to look up the answer in a good bible concordance. No! Jesus fully expected the man to know the written commandment of God, and to understand its meaning. The man recites the first and greatest commandment of God, and the second which is like unto it. Jesus replied, **"You have answered correctly, do this and you will LIVE!"** Jesus added that beyond knowing and understanding the Lord's commandments of love, we must apply them, and live them in our walk of life.

How important is it for the Church to teach and display our Lord's greatest commandment? By the question asked of Jesus, the man's answer, and by the reply of Jesus, our knowing and applying our Lord's greatest command is a matter of eternal life or death! Being a Christian and following Jesus is to follow and trust in His teaching of God's precepts. Therefore, in order to follow Jesus we must know and understand the precepts of God. For Jesus said, He never said nor did anything that did not come from His Heavenly Father. Jesus said, **"For I did not speak of my own accord, but the Father who sent me commanded me, what to say and how to say it. I know that His command leads to eternal life. So whatever I say is just what the Father has told me to say."** (John 12:49.) As Jesus gave of Himself totally unto the will of His Heavenly Father, we too must give of ourselves unto Jesus our Lord, walking in the way He walked. In order to walk as Jesus walked, we must become messengers of the Heavenly King. As disciples of Jesus our lives in speech, and in conduct must reflect the Heavenly Father's will through His Spirit of love.

Chapter Two: "Our Love For God"

"Our love for God" is expressed in proper and pleasing giving.

Giving is a very integral part in being a Christian and expressing "Our love for God." Giving back to God is an expression of our appreciation of what God has given to us. All good things come to us from the Heavenly Father. **"The earth is the Lord's, and everything in it."** (2 Corinthians' 10:26.) Our gracious Lord allows us to share and enjoy the riches of His creation. God supplies all our physical and spiritual needs. Our loving Heavenly Father who feeds the sparrows and clothes the lilies of the field, who loves and cares for us more than these, will supply our physical needs. Our love, joy, and peace are provided by the Spirit of the Lord, and even our faith and hope He provides. Outside of the deposits of Satan some chose to receive, all that we have, and all that we are, is provided by God, and belongs to God. Therefore, every facet of our life should be thanksgiving living unto our Lord. All our giving should be thankful appreciation to our Lord. And all our giving should be done with the thought and hope of pleasing God.

I have given a lot of thought about the gifts of Cain and Abel they presented to God, and the difference the Lord found in them, one gift found the Lord's favor and one did not. Abel's gift was acceptable and pleasing to God. Cain's was not. Why? Abel gave the best of what he had to give. Cain did not. The most important thing we must accomplish in our giving and expressing "our love for God" is that our giving is pleasing and acceptable to God. The great lesson in Cain and Abel, and the indelible impression placed upon us, should be to make all our giving pleasing to God, for having God's favor is the greatest blessing in life. Having God's favor should be the greatest goal and desire of our lives. Abel's gift was acceptable and pleasing to God, and Abel received God's favor and blessings. Cain's gift was not acceptable and pleasing to God, and he did not receive God's favor and blessing. Abel by his giving received everything! Cain by his giving lost everything! "Our love for God," and the outcome of our lives is based on our giving. Due to the magnitude of importance placed on proper and pleasing giving, we must therefore, give our every effort in knowing what we must do to make our giving acceptable and pleasing unto our Lord.

Cain became very angry when God did not look upon him and his offering with favor. **"Then the Lord said to Cain, "Why are you angry? Why is your face downcast? If you do what is right, will you not be accepted? But if you do not do what is right, sin is crouching at your door, it desires to have you, but you must master it."** (Genesis 4:6 & 7.) The only way of mastering sin is to be right with God. When we make Jesus the Lord and master of our lives, and we desire to please Him, our mighty God then will master over our lives. And by the love of His Spirit living in us, He makes our giving pleasing and proper.

We can't repay our Lord for the love, joy, and peace we have received from Him, nor can we repay the Lord, for bestowing life, and life more abundantly, upon His servants who love and serve Him. Our giving is simply a token of thanks and appreciation of God's grace gifts. But, the tokens of our gifts need to be pleasing and acceptable to God. Pleasing and acceptable giving calls for us to examine our hearts, calling upon the Lord to examine our hearts, and lead us by His Word and Spirit, into proper and pleasing giving.

Chapter Two: "Our Love For God"

The prerequisite for proper and pleasing giving is the giving of our selves first to the Lord. Allowing Christ to be the Lord of every facet of our life, is the key to proper and fruitful lives. God's grace and wisdom filling and guiding our lives will enable us to give of our best. When we give ourselves to the Lord, then our giving will come through the grace and wisdom of God's Holy Spirit dwelling within us. For, **"Every good thing given and every perfect gift is from above, coming down from the Father of lights, with whom there are no variation or shifting shadows."** (James 1:17.)

All our giving should come through prayer, and in compliance of God's word, calling upon God's grace and wisdom. **"But if any of you lacks wisdom, let him ask God, who gives to all generously and without reproach, and it will be given to him.** (James 1:5.) We have no excuse for improper giving, only when we jump out front and leave the Lord behind does improper giving occur. Making Jesus Lord of our life calls for making Him master of every facet of our life. God will enable us to give our best through his wisdom and grace.

A number of years ago, I spoke with a man who owned and operated a saw mill in the small town in which we live. He told me that early one morning when he arrived at his saw mill, he found a parked car. Looking inside the car he saw people sleeping. After tapping on the car window, the awakened man rolled down his window. Upon asking the man what he was doing there, the man replied; "We have no place else to stay, our car is all we have." The man and his family were completely destitute. The saw mill owner asked if he would like to have a job. The man replied, that he would. The owner said to the man, " I can offer you a job here at the mill starting today, and I have a vacated house just down the road there that I can furnish for your family." The man was awakened from a night of destitution to having a job and a house for his family to live in.

For the first two weeks the man seemed to be working out well at the saw mill, and his family now had a place to live. But then one day the local newspaper got hold of the story and ran an article on the family and their living conditions. A picture of the living room of the old house appeared on the front page, with the remark that they were having to live on linoleum floors. There was no mention of a man who gave them work and a place to live. Then a group of people from the local churches, feeling the need to help out, began bringing gifts of money, food, furniture, and clothing. Later the man showed up late for work one day wearing a sports coat, and told the owner he couldn't work that day, for he had to carry in furniture. After that he would begin showing up late for work, or not at all until the saw mill owner had to let him go.

My question of the story would be, who gave properly and wisely? Who really supplied the needs of the man and his family? I believe many times our giving, may have been done for the benefit of giving us a good feeling. Giving just to be giving is not proper giving. Our giving should benefit the recipient, and be done in the manner that does not elevate us, and lower the esteem of the recipient. Giving that can build up and encourage others to a better way of life, calls for the love, grace, and wisdom of God seasoned into our giving. Giving to be giving is not good enough. We need to give thought to where the gift is going, the benefit of our giving, and is our giving pleasing to God. We can truly take joy and receive joy in our giving, when our giving pleases the Lord, and the recipients of our giving are benefitted. True appreciation giving unto God demands the giving of our life into God's will, love, grace and wisdom. Giving is a very integral part of being a Christian. Giving through the love of Christ edifies and provides the needs for those in need. True and proper giving that pleases our Lord, carries over into giving God our true worship.

Chapter Two: "Our Love For God"

True and proper worship.

What is true and proper worship of our Lord God?! True worship is this: **"Therefore, I urge you, brothers, in view of God's mercy, to offer your bodies as living sacrifices, holy and pleasing to God—this is your spiritual act of worship."**(Roman's 12:1.) And consider too: **"For those God foreknew He also predestined to be conformed to the likeness of His Son"** (Romans 8:29).

Jesus said these words: **"If anyone loves me, he will obey my teaching. My Father will love him, and we will come to him and make our home with him."**(John 14:23)

Drawing off of these scriptures, we learn that true worship is submitting our selves as living sacrifices to the will of God. To be holy and pleasing to God we must become Christlike. And for the enabling power of the Holy Spirit to live within us we must obey the teaching of Christ. When we stop giving our Lord's commandments and commission first place in our lives, we step out of our love for Christ, and out of His spirit, and into the world. And when we step back into the world divisions occur in our lives and in the Church. Divisions are brought about by worldly people devoid of the Spirit of Christ. (Read Jude 19.) True unity in the Lord's Church, and in our personal lives, and relationships, is dependent upon the Spirit of God's love. Christ is not divided! Within His Spirit is love and unity! True worship of God, and "Our love for God" is to give our bodies as a living sacrifice unto the commandments of our Lord. True and proper worship is not accomplished in a one hour worship service. True and proper worship is accomplished through sacrificed beings into Christ, living every facet of their lives being holy and pleasing to God.

"Our Love for God" is being an Ambassador for Christ!

Are we applying all our God given attributes in "our love for God" by carrying out the mission and position our Lord has given us as new creatures in Christ? As Christians claiming Christ as our Lord, we have been given a new position in life. We find the description of our new position in second Corinthians chapter five verses seventeen through twenty. **"Therefore, if anyone is in Christ, he is a new creation; the old has gone, the new has come! All this is from God, who reconciled us to himself through Christ and gave us the ministry of reconciliation: that God was reconciling the world to Himself in Christ, not counting men's sins against them. And He has committed us to the message of reconciliation. We are therefore Christ's <u>ambassadors,</u> as though God were making His appeal through us."**

"Our love for God" is giving ourselves over to being ambassadors for Christ, becoming messengers of our Lord King Jesus, to whom we have pledged our lives. The earliest known ambassadors carried the message of the king. They were not to speak in their own way, or communicate their ideas. They were to carry the presence and speech of their king. As ambassadors for Christ we are to carry His name, His word, and the light of His presence into a lost and darkened world. As vessels of our Lord's Word and Spirit of love we must carry His message to others, in a proper way. We must never promote our name. Sometimes I hear preachers speak their own names more than the name of Jesus. Good ambassadors never act in their own way. They must always present Christ in His own gentle and humble way. Our hearts should always be after the heart of our Lord. Also, as good ambassadors of Christ, we should never communicate our own ideas, we must be the living word of our King. True ambassadors for Christ are the "Living Bible." I would like to share with you a parable from the "Book of Parables." The story is of a couple ambassadors. Let's read of them and see if we can learn something from them about being a good ambassador.

Claude the Caterpillar and Barney the Butterfly

"I read once of a dashing Knight who longed to rescue his princess, who was imprisoned by a cruel enemy in the palace tower. He devised a plan and recruited two small friends to send her a message. First there was Claude Caterpillar, who was a hard-working fellow but crusty and sour. He started inching his way up the wall toward the distant window, but it was hard work. He grumbled that the sun was hot, causing him to sweat. Then the sun withdrew behind a cloud, it started to rain, and he complained even louder about the raindrops. Finally he heaved himself onto the window ledge, looked at the fair maiden, and said, "Hey, you, come over here. Are you the lady in distress?" She nodded. Claude gave her the once-over and said, "you're kidding." You mean I climbed all the way up here for the likes of you? Well, the Knight says to get ready, he's coming for you at 5:00 p.m. sharp. Think you can remember that, or should I repeat it? And off he went.

Next, the Knight sent Barney Butterfly. Barney, too, battled the rain and the contrary winds. He almost made it to the window when a bird came by and nearly ate him alive. But finally he fluttered in, landing softly on the lady's finger. "Lovely and favored maiden," he said, "the white Knight loves you dearly, and tonight he is coming to rescue you. He asks only that you be ready at 5:00 p.m."

The princess smiled and replied, "Thank you very much, Mr. Butterfly. You are very sweet, and I will be ready tonight when he comes. Claude Caterpillar already brought me the message, but tell me, why was he so disagreeable? He brought me the same news, but after he left I felt worse than before he came."

The butterfly replied, "Oh, you mean Claude? Well, don't mind Claude. That's just the way he is. I used to be that way, too, until I was transformed."

What did you note about these little ambassadors? The following are a few of my notes;

- Claude the Caterpillar didn't carry the love and presence of the knight. He displayed his own personalty, and then he interposed some of his own thoughts, but they were not the thoughts of the White Knight.

- The Caterpillar got out of the role of a true ambassador and the message was lost, for he failed to convey the Knights words and spirit of love to the princess.

- Barney the Butterfly on the other hand, brought forth the words of the White Knight in the very spirit of his love for the princess, and he connected.

- Barney the Butterfly also had a difficult time in carrying out his mission, but never let obstacles nor hardships derail him, nor discourage him from carrying out his mission of the Knight's love.

- Barney the Butterfly was successful because he had been transformed into a beautiful flying spirit of love and kindness.

And if we are to connect with the lost and imprisoned souls of this world, we must carry the word of our King Jesus, in truth, and in His Spirit of love. In order to be ambassadors of our Lord's word and His Spirit of love, in carrying His message of reconciliation, and exalting the name of King Jesus to those He sends us to, we must be transformed by the Word and Spirit of our Lord. We must be transformed ambassadors of our Lord King Jesus in order to express "our love for God."

"Our love for God" must far exceed all others, and all things, in our lives!

Our love and service unto the Lord our God will determine if we are acceptable by our Lord to be His disciples. Jesus and Jesus alone, determines who will be His disciples, and who will receive the gift of His Spirit, and the inheritance of His Kingdom. Just after Jesus had told a parable of the Great Banquet, and how many had refused to attend because they were caught up in worldly matters, Jesus then tells the large crowds that were following Him the cost of being His disciple. If we want to truly express "our love for God," and be in God's Kingdom, we must become a disciple of Jesus, God's Son. In order to be a disciple of Jesus we must hear and understand these strong instructive words that Jesus gives us for being His disciple. We may choose to be disciples of Jesus, but Jesus sets the standards. And in these words of Jesus, Jesus uses a hyperbole to gain our undivided attention and understanding of the price of "our love for God," and the cost of being His disciple, and having a seat at the Great Banquet of Jesus. Here are the words of Jesus regarding what we must do to be His disciples: **"If anyone comes to me and does not hate his father and mother, his wife and children, his brothers and sisters—yes, even his own life—he cannot be my disciple."**(Luke 14:26.)

Jesus sets the terms and gives the example of what "our love for God" must be. Jesus set the living example of loving the Lord your God with all your heart, with all your mind, with all your soul, and with all your strength. And He showed the way of making full submission of our lives unto our Heavenly Father. Jesus has set the terms and showed us the way to being His disciple.

To pick up our cross, crucifying our old self, and fully submitting our life unto Jesus, and the way of Jesus, is the price of being His disciple. Full submission of our lives into Christ is the cost of receiving the full benefits of God's blessings and promises. It is the greatest trade off ever!

- We trade our sins and guilt, for forgiveness and freedom of our spirits!

- We trade death, for eternal life and life more abundantly!

- We trade the burning fires of hell, for the eternal bliss of heaven!

- We trade the state of hopelessness, for a life full of hope, purpose and meaning.

The blessings of being a disciple of Jesus are enormous. Do you know what the problem is of being a part-time Christian? Being a part-time Christian has the same problem as a part-time worker. You don't receive any benefits. Jesus does not employee any part-time disciples, you are either in the world, or out of the world in Jesus, there is no middle ground. All middle ground is Satan's ground. Yes! The price of being a disciple of Jesus is worth it a trillion times over; the reward is immeasurable, but the price set by Jesus, is the price. Jesus' terms are full submission of your love and your life into the way of Jesus, walking with Jesus as He walks.

Encouraging Church members to commit their lives fully unto Jesus as His disciple, can sometimes be a difficult and discouraging task. Sometimes we feel like we are trying to get children to jump from a burning building into the safety net of life, but all they can see is the fear of jumping. They don't see the fires of death and destruction lapping around them. Many refuse to leave what they believe are safe grounds, and commit their lives with a leap of faith into the waiting arms of Jesus, who holds the safety net of life, and life more abundantly. The only thing that keeps us going onward as ambassadors for Christ is seeing those who do make the leap of faith, and seeing their lives transformed into the love, joy, and peace of Christ. And knowing too, that when our testimony seems to go unheard, we do not stand alone, for the Father knows His children and His children hear His voice.

I read a story of firemen arriving at a burning apartment building. By the time they arrived the building was too far gone to be saved. After feeling they had evacuated everyone to safety, suddenly they saw three small children's heads pop up in an open window. They immediately grabbed their safety net, and began hollering for them to jump into the safety net. But, the children were afraid to jump. The firemen and all the people who had gathered around were screaming and pleading for the children to jump, but they still refused. When it seemed all was lost and the children's lives were going to be destroyed by the fire around them, a man came pushing and shoving his way through the crowd, he looked up at the children and said "jump!" And the children jumped from the burning building into the net and their lives were saved. After much cheering and jubilation a fireman turned to the man and said: "Why! After we had pleaded for the children to jump until our voices were hoarse, you said "jump" one time and the children jumped?" The man replied: "I'm their father!"

The Heavenly Father saves His children who learn to love and fully trust Him. We are the firemen doing all we can to save God's children from the eternal fires of hell. As ambassadors carrying out the mission of our Lord, our Lord is always with us. **"Surely I am with you always, to the very end of the age."** (Matthew 28:20.) If we weep over the erring one, we know our Father weeps with us. And we know that our Lord exhausted all His resources to save them.

As firemen for our Lord, our hearts must be on a 24-hour alert! When the Holy Spirit alarms our hearts, we must always be standing in readiness, equipped with the love of God to move into action extinguishing the flaming fires of Satan, saving those who are engulfed by Satan's flames of destruction. And we are equipped too, with the knowledge that the Lord is always there with us, to enable and strengthen us in the battle. Also, He is there to comfort and renew us in our exhaustion.

The battle we fight against Satan and his forces of evil is not just outside the Church walls. A long time ago Satan found out he could not defeat the Lord and His Church, for the Heavenly Father protected them. Satan then slipped in amongst the flock of God, portraying himself as an angel of light, to lead away individual members from the safety of the flock, and their Shepherd. **"For such men are false apostles, deceitful workmen, masquerading as apostles of Christ. And no wonder, for Satan himself masquerades as an angel of light."** (2 Corinthians 11:13-14.) **"When the dragon** (Satan) **saw that he had been hurled to the earth, he pursued the woman** (the Church) **who had given birth to the male child.** (Jesus) **The woman was given the two wings of a great eagle, so that she might fly to the place prepared for her in the desert, where she would be taken care of for a time, times and half a time, out of the serpent's reach. Then from his mouth the serpent spewed water like a river, to overtake the woman** and sweep her away with the torrent. But the earth helped the woman by opening its mouth and swallowing the river that the dragon had spewed out of his mouth. Then the dragon was enraged at the woman and went off to make war against the rest of her offspring----<u>those who obey God's commandments and hold to the testimony of Jesus.</u> (Revelation 12:13-17)

The water and stream represent delusions, religious isms, and philosophical falsehoods spewed from the mouths of Satan's servants masquerading as servants of righteousness, to swallow up the truth in appearance of the truth. Therefore, we are also called into the battle to protect the flock of God. As the preaching/minister I always had a heartfelt desire to protect and build the flock of God, by preaching and teaching God's word of life in His truth, in His love and in clarity, from the palm of His guiding and protective hand. We must, in the spirit of God's love encourage each other to begin our week around the Lord's table, giving praise and thanks to the Lord our God, and learning more of His will for our lives. To me it's important to rise up early enough to have time to begin each day with some quiet time, speaking with the Lord about the new day. Also, I find it important to begin each week in the presence of the Lord and His people. Thomas missed the presence of the Lord after the Lord arose from the grave, because he chose to miss the fellowship of the Lord's disciples. Jesus didn't go to Thomas' home looking for him. Jesus was present where two or three, or more had gathered in His name. Thomas upon hearing that he had missed seeing and being in the presence of Jesus, did not fail to be in attendance the next week when the Church met. And there in the household of God, Thomas got to see and speak with Jesus, and confirm his faith and relationship with Jesus. Jesus told Thomas, **"Put your finger here: see my hands. Reach out your hand and put it into My side. Stop doubting and believe."** Thomas reply and announcement to Jesus were, **"My Lord and My God!"** Then Jesus told him, **"Because you have seen Me, you have believed; blessed are those who**

have not seen and yet believe."(John 20:27-29). Our faith can be shaken by difficult times as was Thomas. Therefore, we must encourage one another to keep the faith, for we walk not by sight, but rather by faith in the Spirit of our Lord. When problems and difficult times arrive in our lives, we must cling to our faith in our Lord, waiting on Him to lift our spirits, and have them soaring high again, like upon the wings of an eagle. We must always keep in mind that all things are possible with God, and that He is the lover of our soul. And knowing too, our Lord can renew us, and make our spirits whole and soaring on high. But we must also remember, "without faith it is impossible to please God."

That is why, as a pastor I always kept an attendance book on all attending members, and when one would miss two sundays in a row I would call on them. My main concern was to make sure they were not hurt, or that their faith had not been shaken by what someone may have said or done. When people leave the fellowship of the Church feeling hurt, and with every passing day that no one calls on them, it just confirms their feeling that they're not cared for there. Most problems can be nipped in the bud when we are willing to help confront the problem. I believe that spiritual and physical growth of the Church comes through those who know and care that those outside of the Body of Christ are hurting and lost! And they are willing to labor for the love and cause of Christ, to encourage His people in their faith in the Lord.

During the first month of a Church in which I served, an elderly mother and her middle-aged daughter attended. When they had not returned in two weeks, I decided to check on them. I found that the mother was a member of the golf course where I played. I asked the manger one day if the lady was on the course. After expressing surprise that she attended church, he told me she was on the 16th hole. When she arrived at the 17th tee box, I was standing on the tee box waiting for her. As she drove up in her golf cart, she looked up at me with a puzzled expression on her face. I said to her, "Do you recognize me?" She replied; "Your face looks familiar." I told her; "I'm the face of the preacher that you told, "I'll see you next Sunday" I haven't seen you in two weeks." Her face turned to shock and then laughter. Over the next year, she and her daughter would be in church every time I called on them and then I wouldn't see them until I called on them again. Becoming a bit frustrated with that situation I decided to call on the daughter to see if I could get a better commitment from her. She told me she had to be home with her mother. I told her you are not with your mother when you are at work and she is out playing golf. You need to tell your mother you have made a commitment to be in church on Sunday morning to worship your Lord. Then tell her she is welcome to come along, and if she decides to stay home, tell her you will see her when you get back. I then asked her if I could read her some words of Jesus? When she agreed, I read her Jesus requirements for being His disciple from the book of Luke. **"If anyone comes to me and does not hate his father and mother, his wife and children, his brothers and sisters—yes, even his own life—he cannot be My disciple."** (Luke 14:26) After hearing the words of Jesus she was somewhat shocked, and replied: "I thought Jesus was a family man!" I told her: "Jesus does care about your family, He loves your mother more than you, He died for her, but Jesus expects you to love Him more than your mother. And He uses this hyperbole to bring to your attention that your love for Christ must far exceed your love for your mother. Jesus made every effort to tell us what we must do to be saved and be His disciples. As His disciples we must be the vessels of God's love, and through His love make effort too win the lost to Christ. Even though not all will chose to follow Jesus, for Jesus Himself wept over those who refused to come unto Him. Therefore, we must not be discouraged, for God cannot use a discouraged person, we must shake the dust off our feet, moving on with God's love, to those who desire the life and love of Christ our Lord.

When we read Jesus description for being His disciple, we must understand there can be no close second places or first places over our love and dedication unto our Lord and Savior. When we elevate Jesus to first and foremost in our lives, all others are elevated as well in our lives and in our love. When we elevate Jesus to first place in our life, our love doesn't diminish for our family, and all whom we know and meet, our love for them increases. God's Spirit of love in our lives will only remain and function properly, when we learn to distribute God's love properly. I once heard an elder say, he knew it probably wasn't right, but his wife was first in his life. We can't give to others what properly belongs to God, and expect to function as a disciple of Christ.

For further emphasis on our Lord's requirements for being His disciple that we found in Luke, (Luke 14:26) let us listen intently to these reiterating words of Jesus found in Matthew (10:37-39). **"Anyone who loves his father or mother more than Me is not worthy of Me; anyone who loves his son or daughter more than Me is not worthy of Me; and anyone who does not take his cross and follow Me is not worthy of Me. Whoever finds his life will lose it, and whoever loses his life for My sake will find it."**

"Our love for God" is expressed by being a bonafide disciple of Jesus, for being a disciple of Jesus is the highest vocation in the world and attainable by all. Whoever places their faith in Christ, and fully submits their life unto Jesus as Lord of their life, they will receive the enabling power of Jesus through His word, and through His Spirit, to live and walk as Jesus walked. To further emphasize the requirements of "our love for God" by being a disciple for Jesus, we need to look intently into Jesus reinstatement of Peter as His Apostle and Disciple, and Jesus' requirements placed upon Peter.

Jesus Requirements, and Reinstatement, of a Fallen Disciple!

"So when they had finished breakfast, Jesus said to Simon Peter, "Simon, son of John, do

Chapter Two: "Our Love For God"

> you love Me more than these? He said to Him, "Yes, Lord; you know that I love You." He said to him, "tend My Lambs."
>
> He said to him again a second time, "Simon, son of John, do you love Me? He said to Him, "yes, Lord; You know that I love You." He said to him, "Shepherd My sheep.'
>
> He said to him the third time, "Simon son of John do you love Me?" Peter was grieved because He said to him the third time, "do you love Me?" And He said to Him, "Lord you know all things; You know that I love You." Jesus said to him, "tend My sheep.(John 21: 15-18)

There is much of which we might glean from the words of Jesus and Peter. What did Jesus mean when He asked Peter, "Do you love Me more than these?" Jesus' words probably covered many things. The other disciples that were there, the sea, Peter's work, his boat, and fishing, Jesus' words meant, do you love Me more than all my creation? And Peter acknowledges that Jesus is an all-knowing God, when he answers "You know I love You." Then Jesus gives Peter a service that encompasses all who are His disciples, "tend My lambs." Could this mean those who have sacrificed their lives into Christ, or His babes in Christ? Take your pick one or both, either way we are to care for those who follow Jesus and place their faith in Jesus; we are always to seek their best interest. The second time around is about the same as the first, except this time Jesus speaks to him as a leader of His people calling Peter to shepherd His sheep. A shepherd always leads his sheep. A good shepherd or leader of the Lord's Church leads by example. They lead in love and mercy, kindness and patience, they walk in the truths and knowledge of the Lord, they lead by following the Word and Spirit of their great Shepherd, Jesus our Lord. The third time around Jesus digs deep into Peter's heart, where Peter's been, where he is at the present, and where he needs to go. Peter's heart was grieved because he knew the Lord knows all things, and Peter knew that the Lord knew his heart was not right. Peter's earlier devotion to the Lord involved self and self-pride. Jesus was now calling Peter into full submission by emptying himself, and fully loving, and serving the Lord his God.

True love and devotion to God, is to deny our self, and lose our self in the Lord's will and Spirit of love. Do we truly love the Lord above all else? Then "our love for God" will lead us to deny ourselves and follow Jesus. "Our love for God," must far exceed all other love. God has cast His love upon us in the greatest display of love the world has ever known, and God pours the Spirit of His love within all who give their hearts to Him. Then the greatest miracle for our life occurs: Christ our Lord, and our Heavenly Father manifest the Spirit of their very being within our lives to enable and empower us to carry out "our love for God," by the power of the Holy Spirit. The glory of God has been shed upon us and within us! The glory of God has been shed upon us and through us in Jesus! And God's glory, the Son of God, has been placed within those who love, and obey, the Lord our God. Should not our love for our Heavenly Father who sent us His one and only Begotten Son, far exceed all other love? And should not our love for Jesus our Lord, who died in our place, and lives for us, and within us, far exceed all other love? Should we not love the Lord, our God, with all our heart, and with all our soul, and with all our mind, and with all our strength? Yes! For, no one merits our love, more than the Lord our God. He is the creator and lover of our souls. "Our love for God" must far exceed all other love! When we fully submit our lives unto Jesus our Lord and Savior, and follow our Lord's commandments and teachings, and when we serve as ambassadors for Christ, carrying forth our Lord's message of reconciliation in His Spirit of love, we show and express "our love for God." "Our love for God" comes by God's love placed in our hearts by the power of the Holy Spirit. God's love is carried out through hearts inspired by His Word and energized by His Spirit. To God be the glory throughout our lives!

"Our love For God"
QUESTIONNAIRE

"Be wise in the way you act toward outsiders; make the most of every opportunity, let your conversation be always full of grace, seasoned with salt, so that you may know how to answer everyone." (Colossians 4:5-6)

#-1. What is the purpose of the short probationary period of life that God has given us here on earth?

_____

_____

_____page 61

#-2. What three truths are required for "true love relationships?" Love must be

_____.

Love must be_____.

and love must be based on_____

_____. page 76-81

#-3. Where do we receive the true spirit of love?

_____.

If we live in love, then _____

_____ lives is us, and we live in

_____. (1 John 4:16-17).

#-4. Why do you think God created you? That His

_____

Might be completed in you (1 John 4:17)

#-5. What will determine complete love, joy, and peace?

Our_____

_____ with God and His children.

John 14: 27—15:9-12. Matthew 25:31-36

#-6. Who opened up their heart to us, setting forth the example for attaining and maintaining "true love relationships?

_____

_____

_____

#-7. For a productive personal life, and church life, how can we put into action the instructions we received from Proverbs 3:5-6? By making every decision in our personal life and in the church through believing

_____, and

following our Lords_____.

#-8. What is love for God?_____

_____. (1John 5:3).

#-9. What is the first and greatest command our Lord gave us to follow?

_____ Mark 12:28-31

#-10. What benefit and promise do we receive in following the first and greatest commandment of our Lord?

_____

Matthew 22:40 & Luke 10:25-28

#-11. For two people to be united as one in the spirit of God's love, what must they do?

_____

(John 17:20-23).

#-12. As Barney the Butterfly, we too, as ambassadors for Christ must be

_____

Why? To carry out our Lord's message in His

_____

Of truth, and spirit of _____

How are we to be transformed?

_____

John 14:21-23. When we get into our Lord's word, and love Him, our Lord gets into us. Then we can fly and soar in the beauty of our Lord's word and spirit of His Love.

#-13. What are Jesus requirements for being His disciple?

_____

_____

_____.

Why did Jesus use a hyperbole in these scriptures?

_____

Luke 14:26-27.

What requirements did Peter have to meet to be reinstated as Jesus disciple?

_____

John 21:15-17

How do we receive the Holy Spirit, the presence of Christ our Lord, and the Heavenly Father in our hearts, to enable and empower us to carry out the good news of Jesus?

JESUS SAID THE FOLLOWING:

"Whoever has My commandments and obeys them, he is the one who loves me. He who loves Me will be loved by My Father, and I too will love him and show Myself to him." (John 14:21)

"If anyone love Me, he will obey My teaching. My Father will love him, and We will come to him and make Our home with him." (John 14:23)

"And hope does not disappoint us, because God has poured out His love into our hearts by the Holy Spirit, whom He has given us." (Romans 5:5)

CHAPTER THREE:
"LOVE FOR ONE ANOTHER"

As we move into the 3rd dimension of God's love, we find "love for one another" the most difficult dimension of God's love. In fact, the third dimension of God's love is utterly impossible to carry out, until we have experienced and received the first dimension of "God's love for us," and have learned to carry out "our love for God," through the Spirit of God's love dwelling in us. God is the provider. We are the exercisers of His love. Without the provision and power of God's love, we cannot complete the 3rd dimension of God's love, nor the divine purpose of our creation.

Charley Brown said: "Lord I have no problem loving mankind, it's the people I meet, that give me problems." I think we can all relate to Charley Brown's statement. We find it very acceptable that God loves us. We love hearing of God's love for us, and of all His promises and blessings He has for us. It is easy to love our Lord who seeks our best interest, and is faultless and perfect in every way. But now to complete God's love, and our divine purpose, we are called upon to "love one another." Actually we are more than called upon, we are commanded by our Lord to; "love one another." One might call this a tough love. It's not easy to love others, and even ourselves, for we are not faultless and perfect people in every way. And we do not always seek one another's best interest, sometimes not even our own.

To overcome Satan's road blocks of resistance to God's Spirit of love, we must first understand the importance placed upon our divine created purpose. We must also know the blessings of fulfilling our divine purpose. The divine purpose for which we were created is to receive and exercise God's love in our lives. We are to return God's love back to God and to one another. When we receive and know God's love for us, and return "our love for God," we then with the Holy Spirit, and the love of His Word guiding us, know and realize that every person is the creation of our Lord, and the object of His love. With the understanding of God's will through His Holy Word, and the Holy Spirit enabling and empowering our life's journey, we can easily overcome the Charley Browns' syndrome. And begin relating more to the lyrics of this popular song of a few years ago. "What the world needs now is love, sweet love, that's something that there is just too little of. What the world needs now is love, sweet love, not just for some but for everyone." The song "What the World Needs Now" became very popular, for it was making a plea to which we can all relate. There is just too little love in the world, too much hate, killing, pain, and hurt. We see that the world needs love, and not just for some but for everyone. Have you ever felt unloved? Probably we all have at times, and it can be hurtful. Have you ever seen an unloved and abused child? Then you have seen the need for love. Had true love prevailed in the world, there would have been no Indian reservations, no slavery, no Holocaust. Yes the song is true. The world needs love, that's something that there is just too little of.

But the real need, the real plea in the song, and in our hearts is really for God. The world doesn't see that, for the world is blinded by the sins of greed and selfishness that keep the world from knowing God, and displaying His love. For God is love. Not only is God love, God is the very source of love! The world catches glimpses of God's love every day, and people see the need. But the world, walking in the blinders of sin, fails to see how the

Chapter Three: "Love for One Another"

love that the world is needing can be in them, and spread through them, if they have a true love relationship with God. Someone needs to show people the way of receiving and giving true love, and that someone is you, Church, the Body of Christ. Within you is the light that can guide the blind to God, and to the way of love. For if God is love and the very source of love, then outside of God there can be no true love. The world needs love. The world needs God!

What the world needs now is God's sweet love, and let it begin in you and me sharing God's love with all we meet. Let the Body of Christ be about learning to love. For if our Heavenly Father commands us to; "love one another" then our love from the Father and for the Father should compel us to love one another. I believe our Heavenly Father would not command us to something without providing the capability of doing it.

THE IMPORTANCE OF KNOWING AND SHARING GOD'S LOVE.

The first step in learning and attaining anything in life, is to see the need of learning, and the benefits of what that attained learning can bring to our lives. The first priority of teachers should be to explain to their students the advantages of learning, for when teachers show their students the advantages of learning, this will instill in them, the desire and zeal for learning and attaining. When we see the overwhelming life saving advantages for walking in God's love, our heart's desire will inspire and compel us into making God's love a priority in our life. Physical exercise has its advantages including our physical well being. A good mental out look, and it can even combat mild depression. Living in a motel room after being transferred, I would sit in my room after work depressed over the move and having to move my family where they did not want to be. One evening I rose up out of my pity chair, and like Forrest Gump I began to run. I did not run as far, nor did I have the following that Forrest had. I only ran a few blocks each evening, but when I returned to the room I felt better and slept better. Physical exercises have their advantages. But far more reaching and beneficial than exercising our bodies is exercising God's love. When we exercise the Spirit of God's love, Then God's love becomes a springboard to our Lord's inner joy and peace in our lives. Also, God's Spirit of Love develops patience, kindness and gentleness toward others. This new abundant life through the

Spirit of Christ, brings to us a blissful life that reaches throughout eternity, when our hearts are energized and ruled by Christ's Spirit of love. Everything else in life pales in comparison to walking in the Spirit of Christ's love. And yet, we should exercise and care for our bodies, for even a greater reason than previously given, they are the temples of the Holy Spirit. Our bodies are like cars; they carry us to work. Our bodies carry our energized spirits of Christ love into our Lord's fields of harvest, where we can work for our Lord. Bodies energized by exercise and proper care, along with spirits energized by the Holy Spirit, exercising God's love, together become gushing springs of God's love in a world thirsting for love.

Once we see the life saving critical need, and the beautiful influence God's love will have upon our lives, and the lives of others, like a runner we will run on and emotional high, never breaking our stride of love. We will sail with the wings of the Spirit's wind under our feet, and in our hearts, carrying us forth across the finish line of displaying Christ, and the spirit of God's love to all we meet. For nothing in life supersedes our knowing Christ and sharing His Spirit of love. Therefore, let us sharpen our minds and inspire our hearts to the importance of God's love by listening intently to the words of Jesus, stressing the importance of knowing and sharing God's love.

Jesus said: **"Love the Lord your God with all your heart and with all your soul and with all your mind. This is the first and greatest commandment. And the second is it love your neighbor as yourself. All the law and the prophets hang on these two commandments."** (Matthew 22:37-40). All of God's laws and commandments were given by God to help create good relationships between ourselves and God, between each other, and within ourselves. Is there anything more important than that? Jesus said the first and foremost thing in our lives is the command to love. The all-important role of our divine purpose in life, of pleasing our Lord, and fulfilling His will, does it hinge on knowing and exercising these two commandments of love? Will the knowledge of God's love, and the way we are commanded to display God's Spirit of love, He has placed in our hearts, fulfill the ten commandments? We find that the ten commandments found in Exodus 20:3-17 are filled when we have the power of God's love dwelling in us. The first three of the ten commandments pertain to God and are covered when we love the Lord our God with all our heart, mind, soul, and strength. When we love God, we will not place any other gods before Him. We will not worship idols, and we will not profane His Holy name. For love always seeks the best interest and welfare of the other. The following seven commandments pertain to keeping the Sabbath day Holy and maintaining a proper relationship with one another. If we love the Lord our God, and the objects of His love, God's Children, then we will keep the Sabbath day Holy, we will honor our parents, we will not murder, commit adultery, steal, bear a false witness against our neighbor, nor covet anything they have. God's love flowing in us and through us covers God's will, and brings rich blessings into our lives. The fulfilling of God's 3-dimensional love in our life, will pave our way over the roadblocks of Satan, and thrust our lives into the joy and peace of our divine-created purpose. Do you want to please the Lord your God, yourself, your family, God's Church, and change the world into a better place? Then make receiving God's love, and sharing God's love the top priority in your life, and then major in it every day.

Clothing ourselves daily in Christ!

How do we go about sharing God's love throughout the day? I like the dress and check system. Making God's love a top priority in our life, and majoring in it throughout the day, calls for us to rise up each morning and cloth ourselves in Christ. Clothing ourselves in Christ and keeping the Spirit of His love properly

Chapter Three: "Love For One Another"

placed, needs the all-important check system throughout the day. When I think of the check system, and of its importance I am reminded of a friend of mine.

When a gentleman friend of ours would occasionally return to visit his mother and father, he would always attend our Sunday School Class. We always looked forward to seeing him and hearing his comments, for he was a highly educated man, and well versed in the scriptures. When he would make a comment on our lesson, everyone would listen. The class was held in the Church Sanctuary; we sat in the back pews. In one of those honored visits, my wife and I were sitting in the pew in front of our honored guest. When our friend began to speak that Sunday we turned, so that we might view him, and better hear him. Upon turning, we saw our friend's tie sticking out of his fly. Evidently he forgot the all-important check system before leaving the rest room, and zipped up his tie in his fly. Suddenly in viewing his tie sticking up out of his fly, the humor of it overcame his intellectual comment. Therefore, his comment failed to connect in the minds of those who saw the tie in the fly. Seeing the humor of the event, we can also see the importance of being properly dressed, and in our friends case that day he needed to employ the all-important check system. Our friend's intellectual comment failed to connect because he was not properly dressed, as we, too, will fail to connect with others, for Jesus, when we fail to keep ourselves properly clothed in the Spirit of Jesus love throughout the day.

When we dress ourselves in the morning it is good to put on the proper attire for the day, do the best with what we have, and get on with our daily business. But, occasionally during the day, one needs to employ the all-important check system. I see women especially, employing the check system, as they pass a window they check their reflection. They fluff their hair in place as their driving down the road. I've had spray flying over on me while driving. Looking over to my wife, I said, "Hey! Hey! What are you doing over there?" She was checking and spraying her hair.

Sometimes our clothing and hair will get out of adjustment, and at proper times, like before leaving the rest room we need to make adjustments. I feel like that would be a proper time for ladies to spray their hair, and for men to check their fly and tie.

When we got out of bed in the morning we would never consider leaving the house undressed, and properly groomed. Even in a rush we take the time to get physically dressed. Although our spiritual well being is more important than our physical well being, we will leave the house spiritually undressed, leaving Christ in the closet of our mind. Christians must rise up every morning and cloth themselves in Christ, filling their hearts with the Spirit of His love, and placing the will of God on the front burners of their minds. How do we do this? By allowing time, quiet time, for prayer, acknowledging Jesus in all our plans for the day, asking Him to guide and direct our day. We must mediate upon our Lord's precepts for it is the teaching of our Lord that makes our pathways straight and true. We then can leave the house properly clothed in His Spirit of love. Throughout the day, we need to apply the all-important check system as we travel along our daily journey, evaluating past deeds, and words spoken during the day. Our check system needs to check out our reflection, are we reflecting Christ? Are we pleasing Christ or grieving His Holy Spirit living in us? Upon a spiritual check of deeds done, and words spoken, were they done and spoken in the spirit of Christ love? We need to take a spiritual rest stop along the way to see if we are fitted in Christ's Spirit of love, and attitude of prayer. The Holy Spirit is with us to help us in being properly spiritually dressed. We might even find we need to back up and make a correction on something we said or did out of the spirit of love, before moving onto a great day in the Lord. Every day should be a great day in the Lord, when we take the quiet time to cloth ourselves in Christ, putting on His Spirit of love, doing everything in love, and making spiritual checks along the way, to make sure we are properly clothed in Christ. The check system also includes the God given ability to think and pray before we act and speak! We need to remember to use our God given ability in every transaction we make. Applying our God given ability will make the day-run smoother, and keep us from the time-consuming embarrassment of backing up and correcting. To ensure proper thinking and prayer before speaking and acting never rush out in front of the Lord, wait upon the Lord, and allow Him to lead in our daily walk. Never rush to judgement, and jump to conclusions, wait upon the Lord and lean on His understanding. Love connects and love conquers, but when we step out of love we disconnect and lose.

How can we make "loving one another" easy? By clothing ourselves in Christ each day, and making spiritual checks along the way, to see if we are following and employing the Spirit of Christ love throughout our daily walk.

Clothing ourselves in Christ calls for the keeping of a wardrobe of God's word in our minds, to cloth and protect us from the elements of the world. We also need hearts filled with God's love which can radiate sunshine and warmth into a dark and cold world. In order to be fully clothed for our daily walks, and a top of the day to you, always rise up in the morning in time for a quiet time with the Lord, clothing your self in Christ before leaving the house. Follow this procedure and the Morning Star will rise up in your heart and lead you in God's love throughout your day. When we allow Christ to rule our hearts, we will remember to apply His Golden Rule.

FOLLOWING THE GOLDEN RULE!

Jesus knew the third dimension of God's love "love for one another" would be our more difficult task of exercising God's love. Therefore Jesus would not only enable us by His presence, and by the gift of God's love, through the power of the Holy Spirit to "love one another," but He also guides and lights our pathway to loving one another, through His teaching. **"Your word is a lamp to my feet and a light for my path."** (Psalms 119:105) Jesus directs our daily path to our "love for one another," through the clothing of our hearts and minds with His teachings and precepts. One of the great precepts of Jesus for guiding our daily walk in loving one another is His Golden Rule. The Golden Rule is also a great check system to see if our conduct toward one another is correct. In our pursuit to "love for one another," and pleasing our Lord Jesus, His Golden Rule must be placed in our hearts and minds, and carried out in our daily walk.

If the Golden Rule were carried out by everyone, the world would be a better place, if not a perfect place. We would get a glimpse of Heaven. If everyone followed the Golden Rule of Jesus, there would be no crime, no police force, no prisons, no poverty, no unloved person. And that is just naming a few of the positives in a world where Jesus Golden Rule is carried out. Do we want to produce positive results in our lives and make the world a better place? Then we must remember the Golden Rule of Jesus and live it out in our daily walk.

The Golden Rule is easy to remember; it's found in Jesus Sermon on the Mountainside, among many other precepts of Jesus, for guiding us into a Christ like conduct. **"So in everything, do to others what you would have them do to you, for this sums up the law and the prophets."** (Matthew 7:12.) The rule is simple and easy to understand. Yet, we might be surprised at how many times we have broken Jesus all-important Golden Rule during the course of the day, if we would reflect back at the end of the day, to see if our words and actions toward others complied with Jesus' Golden Rule.

I preached a thirty minute message one Sunday morning on carrying out the Golden Rule of Jesus. And then I broke my Lord's Golden Rule on Monday. I was driving back from a neighboring town when the car in front of me came to a stop, to wait on cross traffic before making a left-hand turn. A large truck was sitting

Chapter Three: "Love For One Another"

on my back bumper during the stop. When the car made its turn, and I started moving forward, the truck remained inches from my back bumper. At first I thought, this must be someone I know, and they are just fooling with me. It was an eerie feeling. All I could see in my rear view mirror were a large chrome bumper and headlights. I decided to adjust my side mirror to enable me to see up in the cab, so that I might see who was driving. What I saw was a man's face filled with road rage, screaming with anger, shaking his hands, and motioning for me to hurry up. It was a summer day and my window was down, so I promptly responded with a fist pump out the window. And then I slowed down to 35 Mph in a 55-Mph zone. His bumper could not have been an inch off my back bumper, for about a mile down the road. Then when the traffic cleared enough for him to go around me, I could see it was a large dump truck, and the lettering on the door read Carter Trucking. I knew the owner of Carter Trucking, and as soon as I got home, I called the Carters and reported to them what had happened. A few weeks later the owner told me that driver rear ended a car, and that the driver of the car was a lawyer. I said, "Well, don't say I did not warn you." I still need to ask him someday if he was joking about that. But anyway, getting back to the day of the incident, when my wife came home that day I told her of all that had transpired. After hearing my story, she said that I was being smart to him when I slowed down. I told her rather heatedly, "Why do you always have to take the other person's side?" "Did I not just explain to you I slowed down for my safety?" "If he was going to hit me, I would rather it be at 35 mph rather than 55 mph." She replied; "No, you did that to be smart to him, and you broke the golden rule!" And then she walked out of the room. I sulked for about twenty minutes over what she had said, in my mind I grumbled over her lack of support, and attempted to defend myself. After about twenty minutes I walked into the room where she was, and said to her, "You're right! I preached on the Golden Rule on Sunday, and broke it on Monday." I knew in my heart I was not truthful, I had slowed down to pay him back for doing me wrong. I fell victim to what I had preached on the day before. What I said on Sunday was that the Golden Rule was easy to keep and apply toward those who treated you right. The real test comes when someone treats you wrong. The Golden Rule remains the same and still applies when someone treats you wrong. You must treat them in the same manner you want to be treated. I also did the math two wrongs never makes a right. Wrong + wrong = wrong. Wrong + wrong + wrong = wrong throughout infinity. But, wrong + right nullifies wrong, only right can overcome and stop wrong. When we leave the house on our own, unclothed in Christ, the Golden Rule of Jesus becomes impossible for us to live out, as does "love your enemies and praying for them." (Matthew 5:44) Which is another rule among many from Jesus, found in His sermon on the mount.

When we claim Jesus as Lord of our life, along with that claim there must be the obeying of His rules and precepts. What must we do to obey the Golden Rule? We within ourselves are too weak. We must be clothed in Jesus each morning and walk in the enabling power of God's love. Along our daily journey we must give thought and prayer, before we speak and act. A good way of impressing upon our minds to never leave our house unclothed in the Spirit of Jesus, having our hearts and minds clothed in His precepts, is to know and understand the terrible consequences of not being clothed in Jesus. Walking the streets physically naked pales in comparison.

Herein lies the terrible consequence of not walking in the Spirit of Jesus and carrying out His precepts and teaching, we are not His disciples. For, Jesus said, **"If you hold my teaching, you are really my disciples. Then you will know the truth, and the truth will set you free."** (John 8:31-32.) Our lives are bound in lies and deception when we do not hold to the teaching of Jesus. Being a disciple of Jesus is more than carrying a title. Jesus doesn't enter into the hearts and walk with those who simply claim to be

Chapter Three: "Love For One Another"

His disciples. Jesus enters into the hearts of those who love Him and hold to His teaching. Jesus said, **"If anyone loves me, he will obey my teaching. My Father will love him, and we will come to him and make our home with him."** (John 14:23.) Without Jesus we are like an empty boat upon the sea without a Captain, aimlessly adrift without a purpose, and without a destination, waiting for destruction.

I give thanks for the patience of Jesus, for when we on occasion drift out of the sight of Jesus, our light house who guides our path. And for the day I ran out of the house in front of Jesus, spiritually unclothed, and broke His Golden Rule, I give thanks to Jesus for His forgiveness. Help me, Jesus, to never forget, that walking unclothed in Your Spirit brings humiliation to my life. Lord, may I ever be mindful to humble myself before You, to be clothed in Your Spirit, before I begin each new day. For You will never allow me to be ashamed and bound in humiliation by Satan, when You lead my way. I stand in amazement and awe of your teaching, and praise Your Holy Name. All true preaching, teaching, and living must be carried out in the truth and love of Jesus' teaching. Jesus is the teacher. We are the messengers of His teaching, carrying the good news of His gospel message to others in the Spirit of His love. In order to fulfill the teaching of Jesus, which fulfills our lives, calls for our making Jesus Lord of our lives.

MAKING JESUS LORD OF OUR LIVES IS THE DOORWAY TO "LOVE FOR ONE ANOTHER."

Making Jesus Lord of our life is not a one time act of repentance and baptism, even though repentance and baptism are required of us by our Lord to be His disciples. Jesus' first-recorded messages were a call for us to repent, **"from that time on Jesus began to preach, " Repent, for the kingdom of heaven is near."** (Matthew 4:17). Jesus was calling us to a changed heart, and a changed life. Repentance and baptism are the acts of being born again. Jesus said: **"I tell you the truth, no one can enter the kingdom of God unless he is born of water and the spirit."** (John 3:5.) Being born of the Spirit, follows being born of water. **"Or don't you know that all of us who were baptized into Christ Jesus were baptized into His death? We were therefore buried with Him through baptism into death in order that, just as Christ was raised from the dead through the glory of the Father, we too may live a new life."** (Roman's 6:3-4.) Water baptism represents a watery grave where we are lowered and immersed into a grave, making a public statement that we are dying to Christ. As a baby in physical birth breaks through the water to be born, the immersed believer who died to Christ, is raised from the dead, and breaks through the water representing being born again, to walk in the newness of Christ. As Jesus stated in John 3:5, our spiritual birth follows being born of the water. We find examples of the truth of Jesus statements in His own baptism and in our baptism. **"As soon as Jesus was baptized, He went up out of the water. At that moment heaven was opened, and He saw the Spirit of God descending like a dove and lighting on Him. And a voice from heaven said, this is My Son, whom I love; with Him I am well pleased. Then Jesus was led by the Spirit into the desert to be tempted by the devil."**(Matthew 3:16-17 4:1.) **"Repent and be baptized, every one of you, in the name of Jesus Christ for the forgiveness of your sins. And you will receive the gift of the Holy Spirit."**(Acts 2:38.) Having died to Christ and being born into Christ through water baptism and the Holy Spirit, we are babes in Christ. We now have the need as a baby to grow and mature. How do we grow and mature in Christ? We grow and mature in Christ, in the same manner we were born into Christ. We continue daily in the newness of life, walking as Jesus walks, making Him Lord of our life, every moment of every day. When we walk in the way of Jesus, The Holy Spirit supplies the power to love, serve, and honor Jesus as Lord of our life. We must continue each day in our commitment of giving our life to Jesus as Lord of our life, with the same yielding spirit as we did on the first day of our repentance and baptism.

How do we turn ourselves over each day to the divine power of the Lord, now dwelling within us, to lead and direct our daily journey? By getting up each morning and putting on Christ! How do we do that? We put on Christ by allowing ourselves some quiet time with the Lord. During that quiet time we must get into the word of the Lord to know His will for our lives. Begin spending time learning our Lord's commandments of love, and His precepts. Study and learn our Lord's teaching until His teachings fills our hearts and minds. Also, take time at the beginning of each new day for prayer. We must communicate with the Lord about our events of the new day in our daily journey. Then ask the Lord to be with us throughout the day, and for His divine intervention to guide and direct our heart. Then listen to our heart throughout the day. Our Lord directs and guides our lives through His written word, and the Holy Spirit, we must learn to keep attuned to both of them in our daily journeys. If you can only start your day with five minutes of quiet time with the Lord, then devote yourself to that time. For when you see the impact of starting off your day in the study of your Lord's written will, and beginning your new day speaking with the Lord, you will begin to look forward to your quiet time with your Lord. Hopefully your quiet time with your Lord at the start of the day will build to an hour. That would mean rising up one hour earlier, you will not want to do that, until you begin devoting some amount of quiet time each morning with your Lord. And then quiet time with our Lord will be like looking forward to a day of shopping, or fishing, or better yet a day of golf; we awake early, anxious to begin our day with great anticipation. Some of those day's can end with disappointment, when the bargains we hoped for were not there, and the fish were not biting, and our score was higher than all the rest. But the Lord will not disappoint us. There will be bargains galore, we will catch record mounting fish, and we will shoot a low score with birdies and a hole in one, when we make ourselves available to meditate with our Lord at quiet time, and then as we follow Him throughout the day, we will be empowered to a great day, through the enabling power of the Lord's spirit.

" His example"

He lived a life to show the way, that our
lives might not be disarrayed.

So walk with Jesus every day, and follow His Word all the way.

And you will find your life in full array.

Chapter Three: "Love for One Another"

Though much of our days may be routine journeys, we should carry out each daily duty in the Spirit of the Lord, allowing Him to lead our way. Throughout each day we must make ourselves available for the special ministries our Lord wishes to assign to us. Many times our Lord will interrupt our routine daily walk. We are to be available to serve the Lord at all times, even when it interrupts our routine schedule. Much of the time, the needs of God's Children, does not fall into our schedule. We need to learn to fit our schedule into the schedule of our Lord's calling.

I have been called on the phone, and I have been called in my heart into the service of my Lord. One night the Lord called upon my heart, when I was told that Henrietta a member of the Lord's Church Body, was lying at the hospital dying. Henrietta was one of the sweetest spirits I have ever met. She lived alone. She and her husband had never had children, and her husband had been passed away now for some time. I knew that outside of the Lord, she was alone at the hospital. It was a twenty-five-mile trip to the hospital. I was told she was in a coma and she would not know I was there. My heart said, I was her minister and I should be there, even though she might not know I was there. When I arrived at the hospital that night and entered her room, I found Henrietta was lying there alone. I walked over to her bedside and leaned over right above her face, and said, "Henrietta this is Jim, how are you doing?" To my surprise her eyes opened up right in front of my face! And she replied, in the most genuine voice "I'm doing fine, how are you doing?" In my excitement I told her I was ok. Then I asked her if she was hungry, She said that she was. I said, "How about some ice cream?" She said, "that sounds good." I went out and found a nurse, and to her surprise I told her Henrietta would like some ice cream. The nurse sat Henrietta up and we talked while she ate all her ice cream. I stayed until Henrietta fell back asleep. The next time Henrietta would awake, she would be in Paradise. I was glad I responded to the call of my heart. I'm not sure of the purpose I served. I hope it was a blessing for Henrietta before she left her earthly home. I know the Lord had blessed me, for being there with her. I'm glad I was available, and that my heart was attuned to the Lord's call. I'm so glad I did not screen His call, or put Him on hold. Our "love for one another," is being there for one another when our Lord calls upon our heart. Always keep a direct line open to the Lord from our heart.

One night the phone rang around 10:00 p.m.. It was Opal, a lady from the Church. Opal was on Social Security, and she sat with elderly people in need of assistance in their home. Opal's service provided help to people in need and it provided her with extra income. She had called to tell me that the lady she was sitting with was dying. I asked her where she was located. The lady was about twenty miles away from my house out in the country side. I then asked, if she would like for me to come out there and be with her. She replied. "That would be nice if you could." Driving down the dark country road I could see a porch light that Opal said she would turn on. Getting out of the car I wondered if the lady would still be living and what I would find inside. Opal welcomed me as I entered the house, and then took me to the lady. The lady's name was Edna. She was laid back in a recliner and covered up to her chin in a blanket. Opal told me that she had called the family in. One son was traveling in a car from the northern part of the state. The other son was flying in from California. I pulled a chair up beside Edna's recliner and began talking to her. After a short time she responded to me, I asked her if she would like for me to pray for her. She responded by nodding her head that she would. After praying for her I began talking to her, telling her I would be right there with her. As I talked, she began to respond to me, asking my name, after about thirty minutes she asked Opal to help her to the bath room. She said she wanted to comb her hair. Before her first son had arrived, Edna and I were sitting at the kitchen table eating " baloney" sandwiches. Edna was telling Opal to look in the ice box to find me something more to eat. I kept telling her I was fine. Opal was now beside herself, while she

Chapter Three: "Love for One Another"

was happy Edna was doing ok, she kept saying "They're going to kill me for calling them in all this way." She was now becoming more of a problem than Edna. I waited until the first son arrived that I might explain to him what had happened and tell him of Opal's concern. He was very understanding and was happy to see his mother up and going.

I thought about what had happened that night as I drove home. Was it a miracle of the Lord, or was it a well-schemed plot of Edna to get her family home? I guess I will never know. I heard that she moved in with one of her sons. What was my part in all of it? I'm not sure. I just know I was a part of a happy family reunion that night, and I was glad I made myself available when called upon.

The purpose I served in the lives of Henrietta and Edna, I don't know, God knows. I believe the key to carrying out "our love for God," and our "love for one another," is being ready and available when our Lord calls upon us whether it is by phone or through our heart. I sometimes think of myself as a relief pitcher who runs out to the mound to put out the threat when the manager calls. We, as Christians, servants of the Lord, must keep our hearts and minds in readiness, and alert to our Lord's calling. We, too, as Christians must always be prepared in the word and keep our hearts warmed up by the love of the Holy Spirit. Then we will be ready to enter into active service when our manager calls upon us, to put out a threat, and win a victory, for His Kingdom. The Lord knows each of His body member's talents, and how to use them best through the working of His will, as the Lord works out in detail the building of His Kingdom. The greatest and most beautiful temples are not being built by man's architect nor human hands. God is building the most beautiful eternal temple ever built. Our Lord is building it with sweet spirits like Henrietta. Christ is the corner stone, and we, through His Word and Spirit, are becoming living precious stones, being built upon Christ, and mortared together in His Spirit of love. The Lord's spiritual temple is His precious stones rising up in the right hand of our almighty God, declaring the praises of our Lord and Savior, who called us out of darkness, as a glorious lighted temple. It is the empowering hope and the brightly burning light of our Lord's love illuminating out from within us, which overpowers a hopeless darkened world.

CHAPTER THREE: "LOVE FOR ONE ANOTHER"

"LOVE FOR ONE ANOTHER," IS SHARING ONE ANOTHER'S BURDENS.

I have found at times that Christians are very insensitive to the needs of others, due to an old infiltrating religious doctrine. It is a doctrine with which Jesus had to deal with, and one that keeps cropping up today. There is a wide spread belief that whatever happens in your life, or the life of a friend, is always God's will. That sure makes everything simple and easy to understand, and accept. A simple religion taught by the pharisees of Jesus' day, and by the health and wealth teachers of today. The teaching is very simple: if everything is going well in your life, then you must be close to God, for God is blessing you. Therefore, of course, if things are going bad in your life, you must have done something wrong, for God is not blessing you. They judge your faith and nearness to God by your health and wealth. The more you have the nearer you are to God, for God is blessing you. The poor unhealthy person of course is not being blessed, and is not near to God.

Then Jesus came and blew their little religious boat out of the water. The teaching of Jesus went far beyond their superficial religion, when He told them; **"Again I tell you, it is easier for the camel to go through the eye of a needle than for a rich man to enter the Kingdom of God." "When the disciples heard this, they were greatly astonished and asked, who then can be saved?"** (Matthew 19:24-25.) In other words, if the blessed rich can't be saved, then who could? The disciples had grown up under the false doctrine of the pharisees who taught your nearness to God was determined by your health and wealth. Then Jesus delivers a death blow to the Pharisees superficial religion and teaching when He gave to them the parable of Lazarus and the rich man. We find the parable in Luke 16:19-31. Lazarus was a poor man and in poor health, living off of the crumbs of a rich man. As the story continues Lazarus dies, then angels come and carry his soul to the bosom of Abraham in Paradise. The rich man died and his soul went to the lower part of Hades, a place of eternal punishment. To understand why Jesus gave this parable to the Pharisees, we need to look at verses thirteen and fourteen. Jesus said, "You cannot serve God and wealth." "Now the Pharisees, who were lovers of money, were listening to all these things and were scoffing at Him." The parable of a poor unhealthy man going to paradise to be with the Lord, and a rich man going down into the lower part of Hades, a place of torment and being separated from God, this must have blown their minds, and fueled hate for Jesus and His teaching. Jesus followed the parable saying this to his disciples, **"It is inevitable that stumbling blocks will come, but woe to him through whom they come!"**(Luke 17:1.) As followers of Jesus we must be ever cautious to keep in step with the teaching of Jesus. Terrible harm can come to us and others when we take a pathway away from the teaching of Jesus. Our nearness to God is not measured by others, or our wallets, and health. Our nearness to God is measured by the one who can read our hearts and measures the extent of "our love for God," and "our love for one another."

When we were living down in Texas, there had been a lot of rain and flooding. I had read in the paper and had seen on the news, where a Church bus had been swept away by the flooding waters, and many children's lives had been lost. One man whose child had been spared, gave credit to God for sparing his child's life, because he had been into the Word a lot lately. I wondered as I read his statement, how did that make the other parents feel who had lost their children? Did their children die because they were not close enough to God? That Sunday night I was sitting in a Church service, when a number of people stood and gave thanks to God for sparing their homes from the flood. I looked over at Paul whose house was three foot deep in water, and wondered how these testimonies were making him feel? Not only was Paul's house flooded, was he now to believe that God did not favor him? Concerning the man who was in the word of God, and those giving thanks for God's favor being upon them, I wondered whether they had ever read, **"Carry each other's burdens, and in this way you will fulfill the law of Christ."** (Galatians 6:2). I wondered because I never heard in the man's interview any compassion and concern for the parents who lost their children. Nor did I hear anyone mention Paul's name and express concern or offer help in his time of need. The following Wednesday night the minister had asked me to teach Bible study. That night I told the study group I wanted to talk about the testimonies of Sunday night and Paul. After some discussion the group concluded that Paul's house was flooded because they had built his house in a flood zone. The other houses were not built in a flood zone. His misfortune and their good fortune were not due to their relationship with God, but rather circumstances. I hope we can learn to lighten the burdens of others by following the teaching of Jesus and fulfilling His law. Jesus said: **"A new command I give you, that you love one another, even as I have loved you, that you also love one another."** (John 13:34) Jesus' love, the standard of our love, is a sacrificial love that shows concern for the needs of others.

A number of years ago Sandra and I were sitting in a movie theater, when someone came and told us that our friend's Arnold and Shirley's little girl was hit by a car. We had mixed emotions about what we should do. I decided to call their house. I thought if the accident was bad they would probably be at the hospital and not at home. When Arnold answered the phone, I was somewhat surprised and relieved. I said, "We are at the movie theater, and someone came and told us that Dee Ann was hit by a car." I then asked, "How is she doing?" Arnold replied, "She's dead!" I stood in silent shock not knowing what to say, then I finally told him we would be there soon. On the way to the house we rode in silence not knowing what we could say or do. We felt grieved and awkward as we entered the house. We just simply wanted them to know we grieved with them, though we couldn't go where-they were that would come later for us. We don't remember much that was said that night. All I remember being said was Arnold thanking us for coming by. He then said, the last person who had been there told him that this was God's will. I know Arnold did not believe that. But, some thirty years later I still remember those words. The person who made the statement I'm sure made it with the thought that it would help. Years later I had the same statement made to me at our beloved son's funeral, and I can tell you it did not bring relief. I remember my statement to the person who said it, "If God's will were being done in all our lives, it seems to me the Churches would be full of worshipers, we would be living out His will. There would be no drunk drivers running over innocent children, people killing one another, stealing from one another, or abusing one another, if God's will was fully being done in our lives, now would there?

    I don't pretend to comprehend the eternal God who created all things, nor do I pretend to speak for Him. I can only rely on, and relay to others, what God has spoken to us in His written Word. I rely on our Lord's teaching and precepts because I know they are true. My Lord's truth guides my life, and sets my spirit free. I love to share my Lord's precepts with others because I know they are true, and can bring comfort and joy into their life if they are willing to follow them. Trying to speak for God, when a brother or sister is burdened, is not fulfilling the law of Christ. God is fully capable of speaking for Himself. "Love for one another" is sharing the burden of another, feeling their hurt and pain. We don't always have an explanation of why something happens. But we can always share and care as Jesus does. I know that He cares about every tear that falls, even though He did not cause it to fall.

The all-important thing is that we must learn to do is fulfill the law of Christ. One way of bearing others burdens, is to bear them in the same manner we would bear our own. Our burdens and the burdens of others are too great for us to carry alone. When we try to carry our own burdens alone, they will overcome us, and disenable us. We must carry all our burdens, and the burdens of others humbly to the highest power, and cast them upon God. Let us listen to the word's of our Lord's instructions through His written Holy Word, where we are to carry and lay down our burdens.

**"God opposes the proud
but gives grace to the humble."**

**Humble yourselves, therefore, under
God's mighty hand, that He may lift you
up in due time. Cast all your anxiety
on Him because He cares for you."** (1Peter 5: 6&7.)

**"Cast your cares on the Lord
And He will sustain you;
He will never let the righteous
fall."** (Psalm 55:22.)

Along with the preceding instructions of God, we should follow these words of God as an antidote against worry: **"Do not be anxious about anything, but in everything, by prayer and petition, with Thanksgiving, present your request to God. And the peace of God, which transcends all understanding, will guard your hearts and minds in Christ Jesus."** (Philippians 4:6 & 7.)

" In His Hand"

Holding us in the cup of your loving Hand;
May your Spirit of Love flow through our hearts,
Sharing Your gift of Love with one another.

For all hope of life beyond death;
All hope of reunion;
we realize lies in your Hand.

When seasons of distress come our way,
With a cup of grief more than we can bear,
please Lord! Hold us tightly in the cup of
Your loving Hand.

When reasons seem all gone for our going on,
Lift us up Lord; give us reason for our season,
And let us know you hold us in the cup of
Your Hand.

We each have our cups in life to drink,
but we thank you Lord that we may drink them
in the cup of your loving Hand.

We must ask God for His divine intervention, while making ourselves available as the vessels to His divine power. The Lord will enable and empower us through the Holy Spirit and His written instructions, in overcoming our burdens. And now one last instruction for overcoming our burdens, **"Finally brothers, whatever is true, whatever is noble, whatever is right, whatever is pure, whatever is lovely, whatever is admirable–if anything is excellent or praiseworthy-<u>think about such things</u>. Whatever you have learned or received or heard form me, or seen in me-<u>put into practice</u>. And the God of peace will be with you."**(Philippians 4:8-9.) Following the instructions of God, we have now taken the burdens we are carrying to the highest power. We must now wait upon the Lord, act upon His written instructions, and those instructions He writes upon our hearts, and know that everything will be will be all right, for He cares for us. We can now be assured that our burdens will be overcome, for all things are possible with God. The greatest way, and the only way to overcoming our burdens, and fulfilling our life, are to follow the teaching and commandment's of Jesus.

THE NEW COMMANDMENT OF JESUS BRINGS FULFILLMENT TO OUR LIVES, AND COMPLETES GOD'S LOVE IN US.

We find a new commandment of Jesus, in John thirteen, verses thirty-four and thirty-five. **"A new commandment I give you, that you love one another, even as I have loved you, that you also love one another.**

By this all men will know that you are my disciples, if you have love for one another." When "our love for one another" edifies and provides for the needs of others, the world sees the presence and love of Jesus flowing through us. Our lives, the Church, and the world become a better place, where the presence of the Spirit of Jesus Love lives.

Jesus lives through our lives when we place Jesus' new command in our hearts and memory banks to draw on each day, knowing and following Jesus new command will pay our way to drawing near into the Spirit of Jesus. Jesus will guide and direct our daily steps through the power of His precepts and the Holy Spirit in serving and honoring His holy Name. If we are to follow Jesus, the teaching and precepts of Jesus must dwell in our hearts and memory banks. Why? Because the presence of the Holy Spirit of our Lord and Heavenly Father comes into the hearts of those who hold and follow the teachings of Jesus. In fact when we look up the definition of our love for God, it shows that knowing and walking in the commandments of the Lord our God, defines our love. **"For**

this is the love of God, that we keep His commandments; and His commandments are not burdensome." (1John 5:3.) Truly the commandments and teaching of God are not burdensome, they bring great blessings to our lives, from our Lord who loves us. Serving our Lord is following His teaching, and following Jesus brings great honor unto our lives. Jesus said: **"If anyone serves Me, let him follow Me; and where I am, there shall my servant also be; if anyone serves Me, the Father will honor him."(John 12:26.)** The highest and greatest vocation of mankind can be held by all who choose to serve and honor King Jesus as Lord and King of their lives. Jesus is one in the Father. Those who serve and follow Jesus is one in our Lord's Spirit of love, joy and peace. Serving and following Jesus brings to us the greatest reward and honor that one can receive. Our Heavenly Father robes us, and crowns us with His riches and happiness. Through serving and following Jesus our Heavenly Father welcomes us into His Kingdom, here on earth and in heaven. Sometimes we are asked, "Where are you at in your life?" I hope our answer will always be, "I am with the Lord, loving and serving Him." We can only "love one another" as Jesus loves us, through a personal relationship with Jesus. Jesus is the provider of God's Spirit of love, unto those who choose to love Him. By Following the teaching and precepts of Jesus, we are empowered by the gift of the Holy Spirit to love God and one another.

FOLLOWING JESUS IS BECOMING LIKE JESUS!

In order to "love one another" as Jesus loved us, as Christian's we must become like Jesus. True worship of Jesus our Lord is a burning desire to be like Him. Our Heavenly Father in His love for us, not only sent His only begotten Son to die for our sins, He also sent Him to live for us! Jesus before the cross, showed us the way to live by His example. Jesus is the ideal person and child of God that we want to become like. Before the cross Jesus lived for us in the perfect will of God, to show us the way to being a child of God, and having life in the Heavenly Father. After the cross, Jesus and the Heavenly Father, are willing to dwell within all those who love, worship, and idolize them. Through the Holy Spirit we become one in them. The goal and purpose of the Holy Spirit for our lives, is to empower our lives to be like Jesus. Our goal is to walk in the precepts of our Lord and King, by the enabling power of the Holy Spirit, giving honor and glory to our Lord, and our Heavenly Father.

Many Christians who have not fully surrendered to the desire of being Christlike can probably quote to you this Holy Scripture. **"And we know that in all things God works for the good of those who love Him."**(Romans' 8:28). I too love that verse, and it is one of my favorite memory verses. I call upon it during tough times, for reassurance that all will be well, for God is in me, and at work for me. But the following verse, **"For those God foreknew He predestined to be conformed to the likeness of His Son, that He might be the firstborn among many brothers."**(Romans 8:29). This verse is just as important for our learning and understanding, but is not as popularly quoted. Why? Could it be because the popular verse of Romans twenty-eight involves God working for us, whereas the following verse involves us working for God? Someone once said, "many miss success because it is dressed in work clothes." Being a Christian, a follower of Jesus, requires effort and work on our part. Not only are we born into Christ, we are to work to be like Him. How? Disciples of Christ, become like Christ, by walking in the footsteps of His precepts, and through the renewing of our minds. As children who idolize their heroes and make them their role models, whether it is a ballerina or a ball player, children of the Heavenly King, makes Jesus their role model. They idolize King Jesus and make every effort to be like Him. When Jesus says to us, **"Take my yoke upon you and learn from me, for I am gentle and humble in heart."**(Matthew 11:29). Then it should become our heart's desire to have a gentle and humble heart like our Lord's. The yoke of Jesus represents walking with Jesus. But a yoke also represents work! We must make it our daily effort and work to be like Jesus.

The yoke of Jesus also represents a life of service. Being like Jesus and loving as Jesus loved, calls for being a servant of God, and serving those in need. Jesus said of Himself, **"the Son of Man did not come to be served, but to serve, and to give His Life as a ransom for many."** (Matthew 20:28)

I believe some folks miss seeing and walking with Jesus because He was dressed in work clothes. Jesus life was a life of work and service. I believe, too, some miss Jesus and maybe we all lose sight of Him at times, because the attitude of our mind is too lofty. **"Your attitude should be the same as that of Christ Jesus: Who, being in very nature God, did not consider equality with God something to be grasped, but made Himself nothing, taking the very nature of a <u>servant</u>, being made in human likeness."** (Philippian's 2:5-7)

In order for us to walk as Jesus walked, expressing the love of Jesus, we must take on the very nature, and mind set of Jesus our Lord. For us to walk in the Spirit of Christ's love, we must empty ourselves of self, giving Christ full submission into our life, some folks and some carrying the names of Christian are so full of themselves that there is no room for Jesus. To be a Disciple of Christ we must empty ourselves of self, and turn from the ways of the world, and then receiving Christ into our lives, we must strive daily to walk in Jesus' gentle and humble Spirit of love. In the yoke of Jesus we must walk as a servant to the will of God, serving those in need. Greatness in the Kingdom of God is not measured by the worldly measure of who is being served the most. The Heavenly measure is determined by our love and service unto

God and one another. Becoming like Jesus is becoming a servant to God's will and Spirit of love.

Our new birth into the likeness of Christ is a transformation process. Christlikeness comes through a yearning desire to transform our lives into the likeness of Christ. And through the transformation power of Christ's Spirit dwelling in those who love Him and follow His teaching. The call of our Lord to the learning of Him should compel us to work at developing our hearts, like the gentle and humble heart of our Lord and Savior. When we apply the effort and work in learning to become like Jesus our Lord, then the Lord will apply the power of the Holy Spirit in our lives to become like Him. **"And we, who with unveiled faces all reflect the Lord's glory, are being transformed into His likeness with ever-increasing glory, which comes from the Lord, who is the Spirit."** (2nd Corinthians 3:18.) The unveiled faces of which the writer Paul speaks, is the transparency of Christians. Christians are visible to all, by the light of Christ Spirit shining through them. A Christian should be clearly known by their love for each other, and their love and concern for the lost. We should know them individually and collectively as the Lord's Body of ambassadors who are reflecting their Lord's love, and His message of reconciliation. Christians beam on from the light of the Lord's Spirit. Jesus' message that He brought to the world of God's love, and God's message of reconciliation through the blood of Christ, was open, up front, and above board. And those who follow the Lord, the body of Christ, make no secret of their Lord's love and message of reconciliation. True followers of Christ are easily recognized through the transparency of their Lord's message of love. The body of Christ is no secret. The Church is made open to all, and clear to all, to whom they are and to whom they belong. Christians, the body of Christ, hide behind no veil as they reflect the glory of Christ, shining forth the likeness of Christ as they reflect the glorious message of the Lord's love and message of reconciliation. When anyone openly proclaims Jesus as their

Lord, and fully yield unto Him a heart softened to His Word and Spirit, Christ our Lord will mold their hearts into hearts like His, by the creative power of His loving gentle Hand. To "love one another" as Jesus loves us, comes through a transformation process of our learning of Jesus, and the glory of Christ's Spirit developing us into His likeness and Spirit of love. Yes! Christianity is much more than a religion; true Christianity is developing a personal relationship with Jesus, through our desire to know and love Him more, and by the power of the Lord's connecting Spirit of love, making us one in spirit. And even more true, Christianity is a transformation into the likeness of Christ. Yes, Christians should be transparent for all to see the Spirit of God's love shining through them.

LEARNING TO "LOVE ONE ANOTHER" AS JESUS LOVED US.

In order for us to love one another as Jesus loved us, we must look and learn of the manner in which Jesus loved us and then begin exercising the same manner of our Lord's love toward one another. For the manner in which Jesus loved us, we must look into the great love chapter on God's love: first Corinthians' chapter thirteen, and we must look to the cross of Jesus. Christ's love for us produces outward signs and actions that we must show toward others. The two great defining virtues of the outward signs of God's love, and the indwelling of the Holy Spirit we find in God's word are:

"LOVE IS PATIENT."

The patience of our Lord's love showed to us, went far beyond the measurement of our minds, when forbearing the pain and agony of our sins upon the cross, Jesus said, "Forgive them Father for they know not what they do." Patience is the forbearing and putting up with the sins and wrong doings of others. When I look upon the cross and see the patience of Christ's love for us, I know He expects us to exercise patience toward one another. We know this by our Lord's command, "Love one another. As I have loved you, so you must love one another." To love as Jesus loved, we must be like Jesus in showing patience to our brothers and sisters in and out of Christ. And if we have a problem in exercising the patience of God's love toward one another, then we must go to the foot of the cross of Jesus, and listen to the words of our Savior. Jesus while bearing each of our sins in His body through suffering anguish speaks these words: "Forgive them Father for they know not what they do." Jesus in loving patience was forbearing in His own body, the ignorance of our sins, in order to save us from those sins. Patience is a virtue of God's love that shows forth mercy. If we desire mercy from our Lord then we too must be merciful. God's love produces patience, mercy, and kindness that win us over, and draws us near unto Him. Therefore, if we are to be like Christ, and win others to Christ, we must exercise patience and kindness toward others. We must become vessels filled with the

Spirit of Christ, from which the gentle Spirit of His love flows forth patience and kindness to others.

There should never be a question pertaining to what the love of God is, for God defines His Love for us. In the great love chapter, (1 Corinthians 13:4-7) we find a list of virtues that God's Love produces. And first on His list of virtues is "patience." Patience is not an easy virtue to have and display, and without the power of God's Spirit of Love, patience is utterly impossible. One of my favorite people, my old friend Ed Risinger, was the epitome of our Lord's patience and humbleness in our community. Another friend of Ed and myself, Tom Smith, who attended the same Church that Ed attended, told me that one layman Sunday Ed spoke on the virtue of humbleness. If anyone was ever qualified to speak on patience and humbleness in our community outside of our Lord, it would have been Ed Risinger. Ed also had another virtue that of listening and giving thought before he spoke. Learning to listen and giving discernment before speaking, comes from exercising one of the products of God's virtues "patience." The virtues of God's love are the necessary components for a finished eloquent speaker. Tom said, during Ed's message on humbleness, Ed paused for a moment in thought, and then said: "Humbleness is a strange virtue. It is difficult to attain. For once you think you have attained it, then you haven't." Ed never thought he had attained humbleness, and he had. Being a godly man, Ed displayed the spirit of our Lord's virtues of patience, gentleness, and humbleness. Ed Risinger was a role model of our Lord's spirit living in man, to me and the community in which he lived.

I have given a lot of thought as too why God listed patience as a virtue. I also wondered why God would give patience such prominence as to place it first on His list of virtues? When I begin to give thought as too why patience, is such an important part of walking in God's love, I discovered the following:

<u>First</u>, -I discovered that I was thankful God had been patient with me, for having walked in my own willful way, against the will

of God, for twenty-seven years. In my rebellion and foolishness I thought that I knew more about living life, and having fun, than my Maker, the Creator of life. What an arrogant piece of work I was, for God to put up with, my life is proof that God in His love for us, is merciful and patient. I came to discover that God desired to provide for me, and all His created children, life and life more abundantly through Jesus. After discovering this in my life I then began to be more thankful for the patience God's Love gave to me, and how much I needed God's patience and still do. I pray that as I grow in the Lord each day I will realize the need and power of God's patience, produced by His Spirit of love. Each day I will strive to make myself available to His presence and the guidance of His will by following the teachings of Jesus and walking in His Spirit of love. But when I do fail I know my Lord will be there to pick me up, dust me off, and put me back on His narrow and straight path of truth and righteousness through His patience.

<u>Secondly</u>, -I discovered and realized that if I needed and wanted the patience of God, and the patience of others, I myself needed to show patience. For after all, I should understand the need of tolerance and patience for others, since I had taken all of twenty-seven years to acknowledge the need of Jesus as my Lord and Savior. I then began to think I should stop wondering, and no doubt stop telling others in a sense, why are they so foolish as not to see their need for the Lord. Though I do wish at times that I had not been so foolish. And I do wish at times that someone with the love and patience of God would have taken the time, to explain to me at an early age, why I should have made Jesus my Lord and Savior. I think of what a great positive difference that would have made in my life, and the lives I affected. To walk as Jesus walked, and to be an effective witness of our Lord, we must be a display of His Love and Patience.

<u>Thirdly</u>, -When we look back over the mistakes and sins of our lives, and begin to listen more to other people's stories, of the

CHAPTER THREE: "LOVE FOR ONE ANOTHER"

mistakes and sins they have committed, tracing back, we find that many times the cause of our sins came about through our lack of patience. As we read the word of God, at times questions will arise. Though we know God's word is true, sometimes we must search out the truth. When we give time in searching out the truth of God's word, it becomes much more meaningful. Having questioned why God listed patience as the first virtue and product of His love, and having searched for the truth of why patience is that important, we can now see clearly why we must develop the virtue of patience out of God's love. Because a lack of patience showed to others, leads to a chain of other sins, like rudeness, unkindness, and unrighteous anger, just to name a few. Many of our sins against others are born and bred by our lack of patience. Patience guards against sinning against God and others. Though all sin is against God, sometimes our lack of patience is directly against God. Many of our failures and sins in life are a direct result of not waiting upon the Lord. When we surge ahead of our Lord's divine direction, and intervention, tragedy awaits us. Our desire and the empowering love of God to produce patience in our life, is one of God's greatest blessings for our lives, and for the lives that we touch and affect. Knowing now of the spiritual greatness and accomplishments of patience, we should ever strive to develop the virtue of patience in our lives, through the power of God's love, and our desire to be like Christ. Patience is the love of God. When we display patience and kindness toward one another, we show the spirit of, "our love for one another." The second listed outward sign of God's Spirit of Love, and the indwelling of the Holy Spirit within us is the virtue of kindness.

God's Love In 3-Dimensions

"Love is Kind."

Do we not know it was the kindness of God's Love that brought us to repentance, and gave us a new life? **"Or do you show contempt for the riches of His kindness, tolerance and patience, not realizing that God's kindness leads you toward repentance?"** (Romans 2:4.) **"Consider therefore the kindness and sternness of God: sternness to those who fell, but kindness to you, provided that you continue in His kindness. Otherwise, you also will be cut off."** (Romans 11:22.)

I hear many express that God's love is unconditional. God is no respecter of persons, which the scriptures clearly state. I love this about God; God sets the standards and they are fair for everyone with no exceptions. When we say God loves us unconditionally, are we saying God accepts us on any level? Or does God set a perimeter on His love and kindness? Read the previous verse from Romans chapter eleven; do you see a condition on God's kindness? Let us dig a little deeper. God's love expressed through His only begotten Son on the cross at Calvary, I believe to a point was unconditional. "For God so loved the world that He gave His one and only Son," God gave His only begotten Son, and Christ died for all. That act I believe is unconditional love, whether we choose to accept it or not. God's love for each of us, sacrificed His only begotten Son for each of our sins. But now as Paul Harvey would say, for the rest of the story. The rest of the story, or promise says, "that whosoever believes in Him shall not perish but have eternal life." In these great and familiar words of Jesus we find a condition placed on God's love and sacrifice for the world. Throughout the scriptures we will find it to be true that God places conditions for us to remain in His love, and for His love to remain in us. **"As the Father has loved Me, so have I loved you, now remain in My love. If you obey My commands, you will remain in my love."** (John 15:9 & 10.) These are the words of Jesus. Again as we found in Romans chapter eleven verse twenty two, God's love will continue to express kindness toward us, if we continue in His kindness.

In this probationary period in which we are living God has cast His love upon each one of us through Jesus. In patience and kindness our Heavenly Father now awaits our decision to accept or reject His love. For those who refuse to open their hearts to Jesus, and receive God's love, God's sternness of His judgement and punishment awaits them. But! For those who choose to receive the love of God, and walk in the attributes of His spirit expressing patience and kindness to all God's children, the lost and the found, the kindness of God continues upon them! Not only does God's kindness continue upon us, the very presence of the Holy Spirit of the Heavenly Father, and Jesus our Lord dwells within us. The presence of the Holy Spirit dwelling within us lifts and thrust our spirits to heavenly realms on high. Our spirits will fly and soar as an eagle, by the power of the love, joy, and peace the Holy Spirit brings into our lives. The choice of receiving God's Spirit and gift of love has been given to each of us, through the love and sacrifice of Jesus our Lord and Savior. The choice is ours, which shall we choose, the sternness of God, or the kindness of God? The love of God created us as free will beings that we might choose to accept or reject His love. Why? Because, I believe, God was seeking true love relationships with us, and a true love relationship calls for voluntary choices on the part of each party. Those choices include the choice to receive God's love, the choice to return God's love, the choice to share the spirit of God's love with one another, the choice to continue in God's patience and kindness through the gentle and humble heart of Christ. The empowered life of God's Love comes through the choice to accept Jesus, God's gift of love and grace, as Lord of our lives.

"Our love for one another" through the gift of God's love expresses patience and kindness toward one another. When we stop and think about it we never have an excuse to be rude to another person. As we think on that, let us think of the Golden Rule our Lord gave us to apply throughout our lives. In the boundary of the Golden Rule there lies no rudeness. Christians are out of bounds when they are rude to another. Kindness toward others must prevail in the Christian's life.

"Love for one another" as Jesus loved us, can only happen through God's love producing virtues. As we look intently into the virtues that only God's love can produce, we will see a great need within ourselves, and within our society, for people of high integrity. People of high integrity are undivided in their love for God, and their love for His precepts in living out their lives. We must completely understand that a virtuous life is only produced by a heart filled with God's love. And we need to know too, that only God, the source of love, can fill a heart with love. Our only hope of stopping the moral decline of the world is to produce people of high integrity whose hearts are filled with love. And our hope does not disappoint us, for God is willing to pour out His love into our hearts through the Holy Spirit. As a society we must somehow see the great need for God's gift of love, and begin exposing ourselves and our children to God. Throughout the Holy Scriptures we are instructed to seek God. And we must know God rewards those who earnestly seek Him. The Heavenly Father waits for His prodigal children, with open arms of love, that He might fill their hearts with His love, and the riches of His virtues.

We have already emphasized the importance of the two great virtues of patience and kindness that God's love produces in our lives. But it would be remissness for us to not look into the entire Holy Scripture's description of what God's love produces, and does not produce. **"Love is patient, love is kind. It does not envy, it does not boast, it is not proud. It is not rude, it is not self-seeking, it is not easily angered, it keeps no record of wrongs. Love does not delight in evil but rejoices with the truth. It always protects, always hopes, always perseveres."** (1 Corinthians 13:4-7).

Having looked into the entire descriptive list of what God's love provides, we must also consider what a heart filled with God's love does not do. For God's list of do nots are warning signs to prevent us from entering into life's dangerous hazards. Here is a list of what love does not do: "love does not envy." To envy another is to covet what God has provided them. Envy is breaking God's 10th commandment **"Thou shalt not covet."** When we envy another, we remove ourselves from "Love for one another." We also remove ourselves from thankfulness unto our Lord for our provisions that He provides. "Love does not envy." Also, "Love does not boast." Any boasting from a child of God should be in the form of praise for their God. For all good gifts come from the Heavenly Father. Therefore, any acknowledgment of our gifts, whether they are personal or material holdings, they should be acknowledged in the form of praise and thanksgiving unto our Lord. For one to boast is an effort to raise their self above others. For one to boast is to dismiss their God, and their "love for one another." The ground at the cross of Jesus is level and humble ground, for we all need a Savior. Next we find that "Love is not proud." Pride proceeds the fall, as it did in Lucifer who became proud, and boasted that he could become higher than God. God's love lifts us up, but pride casts us down. Pride removes us from the grace of God, for, **"God opposes the proud but gives grace to the humble."** (James 4:6). "Love is not proud." And too, "love is not rude." As previously mentioned there is never an excuse for a child of God to be rude to another person. When we become rude, we step out of the boundaries of our Lord's Golden Rule. "Love is not rude." We now find that, "Love is not self seeking." Love seeks God's own level, which reaches far above ourselves. Our love should always seek the best interest of our Lord and Savior. And our love should always seek the best interest of others. "Love is not self seeking." Also, "Love is not easily angered." When we become easily angered, it usually results from our being touchy about us, and our self interest. Unrighteous anger does not serve the will of God. Be slow to anger for, "Love is not easily angered." Though we have reached the last listing of what love does not do, it is far from the least of importance. "Love keeps no record of wrongs." Due to the special emphasis that Jesus has placed on forgiveness, we must therefore, place as much understanding and application to "Love keeps no record of wrongs," as we do to the virtues of patience and kindness.

"LOVE KEEPS NO RECORD OF WRONGS."

I spoke to a young man one day after a funeral service about his need to become a Christian. The young man's mother was a good Christian lady and a member of the congregation where I was serving as the preaching/minister. I knew she was concerned about her son, as all Christians should be concerned about those outside of Christ. In our brief conversation, due to our lack of time, I gave him just one reason as to why he should become a Christian. The one reason I chose to give him was the great blessing of "Forgiveness." In order that we might be forgiven, and for us to be forgiving of others, comes only through the empowerment of God's Spirit of love. The great blessing of being forgiven, and the power to forgive others, comes only to those who fully submit their lives to Christ and become a Christian. I spoke to him of how great the blessing is of having a spirit free from sin, which comes from being a Christian. I then told him of why that only God can forgive us of our sins. And that only through God's Spirit of love can we forgive others as He forgives us. He then shared with me that he could not forgive some people. I then told him, outside of Christ you will never be able to forgive, and be forgiven, your spirit will be bound by your sins and by the animosity you are holding in your heart. For only Christ can free us of our sins, change our hearts, and set our spirits free. In order to receive the great attributes of joy, peace, and a free spirit we must be forgiven and we must be forgiving. For freeing our spirit of the record of sins that God holds against us, and the sins that we are holding against others, we must accept Christ as our Lord and Savior. I wish I could tell you he accepted Christ into his life then and there. But maybe a seed was planted, and maybe someday, someone will water that seed, and he will accept Christ as his Lord and Savior. Then he will know the great blessing and empowering virtue of "Forgiveness," and the joy and peace of a free spirit.

One cannot express in words of the joy and peace that comes into your life, when all record of sin and animosity has been wiped clean from your life, by the love and blood of Jesus. For, "Love keeps no record of wrongs." Jesus gave to us some strong emphasis as to why we should hold no record of wrongs. Jesus did this in His model prayer that he gave to us to pray daily. Jesus told us to pray in this manner "Forgive us our debts, <u>as</u> we also have forgiven our debtors." The instruction of Jesus our Lord, becomes very clear, that in the divine order of God's forgiveness, we will be forgiven in the very same manner that we forgive those who trespass against us. In all of the instructions, our Lord gives us in how to pray, only on "Forgiveness" does He place such strong emphasis. We find the strong emphasis Jesus places on forgiveness in the verse following the Lord's Prayer.

"For if you forgive men when they sin against you, your Heavenly Father will also forgive you. But if you do not forgive men their sins, your Father will not forgive your sins. (Matthew 6:14-15).

Only God can forgive sins. Only God can change a heart. And only God can pour His Spirit of love into a heart through the power of the Holy Spirit. Love overcomes the sins that we commit, and the sins of others that we hold in our heart. "Love keeps no record of wrongs." The act of forgiveness is divine, for it is produced by the Spirit of God's love.

Do you want "True love relationships?" Then exercise God's gift of love. Love is patient, love is kind, love is forgiving. Do you want to make your life miserable and your mates miserable? Then never forgive, never forget, just keep digging up old bones and throwing those old wrongs at them. Jesus said, we are to forgive as we have been forgiven, we are to love as He has loved us. To walk as Jesus walked, we must walk in His Spirit of love. His **"Love does not delight in evil but rejoices with the truth. It always protects, always trusts, always hopes, always perseveres. Love never fails." (1 Corinthians 13:6-8)** The indwelling Spirit of God's love, producing the virtues of patience, kindness, and forgiveness, protects our need for Christ living in us, and for true love relationships in our lives.

What are the signs of one having the Holy Spirit? What are the expressions of the Holy Spirit in our life? Are the expressions and signs of the Holy Spirit in one's life found on bumper stickers, crosses around our necks, or speaking in unknown tongues? Jesus has the answer to these questions and all our questions. What are the signs and expressions of one having the Holy Spirit dwelling in them? Jesus who is the giver and sender of the Holy Spirit into our lives said this: **"If anyone loves me, he will obey my teaching. My Father will love him, and we will come to him and make our home with him." "By this all men will know you are my disciples, if you have love for one another."(John 14:23.)** By Jesus own words, the sign of the indwelling of the Holy Spirit is love and obedience to God. Also the expression of patience and kindness toward others, are signs of the Holy Spirit dwelling within one. The signs of the indwelling of the Holy Spirit are expressions of God's Love coming from our hearts. Let us never lose sight of where our focus in life should reside.

With the Cross of Jesus Ever Before Us, Our Life Resides in God's Love!

We must make every effort and take every precaution to follow our Lord's new commandment of loving one another as Jesus loved us. One of those daily efforts and precautions is to look upon the cross of Jesus. There upon the cross of Jesus, we see the fullness of Jesus' love for us that we are to share with one another. Do we see Him now bearing for us our cross of agony, our shame and guilt, and dying for us, that we might be free from sin and death? We see our Savior's love upon the cross being not only for us, but for all those that we meet each day. For all that we meet each day, and for all the Lord sends our way, our Lord's love was willing to endure our sins, and sacrifice Himself for our needs. "Our love for one another" must be as our Lord's. The love of our Lord calls for patience in putting up with the mistakes and sins of each other, and for the kindness that reaches out to the needs of others. Jesus' love fulfills our needs and seeks our best interest, through the fullness of Jesus' love He shared for us upon the cross, He calls for us to share with one another. The love of Jesus that we see displayed for us, reaches far beyond human capabilities. Our capability to love one another, as Jesus loved us, is enabled and empowered by God's Love poured into our hearts through the Holy Spirit. God is the provider of love; our part is never to grieve the Holy Spirit by failing to exercise the gift of God's Love, by loving all those we meet in the manner Jesus would love them.

Unveiling God's Love!

When God plants the Spirit of His Love into our hearts through the Holy Spirit, and we nourish God's Spirit of Love with His Holy Word and fervent prayer, our love grows. While love is the unseen indwelling Spirit of God, love unveils itself in many visible forms. "Our love for God" reveals itself in fond affection for studying God's word, and through our fervent prayers to God. Our hearts and minds are relay stations of what enters into them, bad stuff in bad stuff out, good stuff in good stuff out. When we allow God's Love to fill our hearts in Christ, the beauty and greatness of God's Love flows out of our hearts to God. Our love unveils itself in a great affection of warmth, feeling and enthusiasm of our heart, mind, soul and strength toward God and His perfect will.

"Our love for one another" unveils itself and becomes visible to others through fond affectionate speech, and deeds of kindness toward one another. Our love also reveals itself when we show patience that puts up with and forgives the sins and mistakes of others, as well as our own. Our love becomes visible to those we know in affectionate speech, writings, handshakes and hugs. Love always unveils itself to others when we carry out the will of our Lord in our daily walk. **"And so we know and rely on the love God has for us. God is love. Whoever lives in love lives in God, and God in him."** (1 John 4:16.) Living in and displaying the Spirit of God's love, is the outward sign of the indwelling of the Holy Spirit.

The first fruit and the greatest gift of the Holy Spirit is love. The Holy Spirit like love is an invisible feeling that dwells within. The Spirit's gift of love unveils itself to others through acts of patience, kindness, and gentleness. The Spirit also unveils itself to God in faithfulness and praise. Our love for God, unveils itself in prayers and songs of praise. Our love for God, is also revealed through faithfulness in following God's teachings, and through testimonies that glorify His Holy name. And so we rely on the indwelling of the Holy Spirit to convict and direct our daily walk with Jesus. The Christian's daily walk is to be affected and influenced by God's Spirit of Love. The Christian's speech, actions and transactions with others should be done through forms of unveiling love. Jesus is the great unveiling of God's Love. We, too, as disciples pleasing unto our Lord, must be the unveiling of God's Love.

Our Goal and Destiny

Our destiny is heaven. Our goal is to please our Lord Jesus Christ. The ticket to our destiny is a heart sealed and delivered into the likeness of Christ. During this probationary period of life, we each have been given the choice of our destiny. Jesus came to show us the pathway of truth that leads to life more abundantly and eternal life with our Heavenly Father. Jesus is the roadmap and pattern to truth and life. Jesus stands at the crossroads of life, and says, "follow me." Following Jesus is through a spiritual realm, and within that realm is the direction of our Lord's Word, the power of the Holy Spirit, and within that realm, Jesus develops the hearts and minds of those who desire to follow Him into His likeness.

Our part is to follow and thirst after the likeness of Jesus. Our desire and thirst to be like Christ will increase with every step we take down the pathway of Jesus likeness, as each step brings us into a better view of the goodness and beautiful glory of a Christ likeness life. With every step down the pathway of life into the likeness of Jesus, our desire will increase for having Jesus mold our hearts into the gentle and humble likeness of His own. And then as we begin to walk in our Lord's own gentle way, and feel the glory and peace that His gentle Spirit brings our way, our hearts will leap with the joy and desire to walk in a gentle way that is evident to all. The peace of a gentle and humble heart that only Christ can mold, will become more desirable than all the treasure and pleasure this world can afford. For nothing can surpass nor even compare to walking with Jesus in His own sweet Spirit. The feeling of walking in the Spirit of Jesus will be our heart's desire.

And then as we see the benefits and strength Jesus' precepts and teaching offers into our life, our walk of life will glide on a spiritual high. When we learn to love the Lord our God with all our heart, with all our soul, with all our mind, and with all our strength, our life enters into a closer walk with our empowering Lord and Savior. And when we learn to love each other as Jesus loved us, our walk with our Lord becomes an empowerment walk of faith that gives strength to others in their walk of faith in Jesus. Not only are we to receive the power and strength of our Lord's Spirit of love, we are to share the strength and power of His Love with one another on the upward pathway of life. Jesus' love compels us to reach out for the wayward, and the faint of heart, bringing them into the strength of our Lord. Therefore, let us build up and encourage one another, cheering each other along the upward pathway of life, fastening our eyes on Jesus, seeing and feeling Jesus glory and Spirit of Love more clearly with each upward step we take. Always looking up to others on a higher plane for encouragement, and back to others to cheer them onto a higher plane in Jesus, until we all cross the goal line of being like Christ.

The destiny of being with our Heavenly Father in heaven, awaits those who fulfill their created and designed purpose in life.

God's Love In 3-Dimensions

In order to have and know the fullness of life, we must complete our designed purpose, which is the completion of God's Love. When we choose to open our hearts and receive God's love, then choose to return God's love by loving the Lord our God, with all our heart, mind soul, and strength, and then share God's love with one another as Jesus loved us, we walk in the fellowship of Jesus our Lord, and the Heavenly Father, and the Children of the Heavenly King. Life is complete when we walk in the 3-dimensions of God's Love. When we receive the Spirit of God's love, then return the love of our Father in Heaven, and love one another as Jesus loved us, then God lives in us, and His love is made complete in us. The greatest gift, and the greatest and most significant news given to us, that we have to share is, "God's love for us." When the rising Morning Star, God's gift of love, rises in our hearts, the world becomes a brighter and better place by the presence of God's Love, Joy, and peace aglow within us.

As we sojourn here on earth, and walk in the love of Jesus, with the Heavenly Host cheering us onto victory, let us ever strive to a life of victory in Christ by remaining in God's Love. May our travel through earth leave a trail of love and peace for others to feel and follow, as our love for God elevates us to our Heavenly dwelling prepared for us by Jesus our Lord. All praise and glory are given unto the Lord our God, who enables and empowers our flight through His Spirit of Love unto our promised home. The promises of Jesus give encouragement and an empowerment walk to all who overcome the world through Christ their Lord. Let us hold our Lord's promises in our hearts and minds to ever be true. **"I will live with them and walk among them, and I will be their God, and they will be my people."** (2 Cor. 6:16.) **"Him who overcomes I will make a pillar in the temple of God. I will write on him the name of My God and the name of the city of My God."** (Rev. 3:12.) **" He will wipe every tear from their eyes. There will be no more death or mourning or crying or pain, for the old order of things have passed away."** (Rev. 21:4)

Chapter Three: "Love For One Another"

The promises that the Lord our God gives, to those who love Him, is an exemplification of "God's Love for us." God's love is the victory that overcomes the world and sets our spirits free unto a Heavenly flight through a life of love. May the promises of our Lord be with you, and His Spirit of Love direct your life's journey unto a higher plane that overcomes the world, and you will soar into the Heavenly realms of God's Love, that brings peace and joy unto your life.

May God bless the writing and reading of this book, and may all our praise and glory be given to our Heavenly Father, and our Lord and Savior King Jesus, for life and life more abundantly through "God's Love in 3-Dimensions."

I would like to ask you to pray for our family, and for our ministry in our Lord's Kingdom. In closing I will pray the Apostle Paul's prayer for you found in Ephesians 3:14-21.

"For this reason I kneel before the Father, from whom His whole family in heaven and on earth derives its name. I pray that out of His glorious riches He may strengthen you with power through His Spirit in your inner being, so that Christ may dwell in your hearts through faith. And I pray that you, being rooted and established in love, may have power, together with all the saints, to grasp how wide and long and high and deep is the love of Christ, and to know this love that surpasses knowledge–that you may be filled to the measure of all the fullness of God.

And now to Him who is able to do immeasurably more than all we ask or imagine, according to His power that is at work within us, to Him be the glory in the church and in Christ Jesus throughout all generations, for ever and ever! Amen."

"Our love for one another"
Questionnaire

"But in your hearts set apart Christ as Lord. Always be prepared to give and answer, to everyone who asks you to give the reason for the hope that you have. But do this with gentleness and respect." (1 Peter 3:15)

1. What is the importance of knowing, and sharing God's commandments of love through God's Spirit of love? Knowing and sharing God's love fulfills all the

_____

_____

_____. Matthew 22:37-40.

#-2. What is the importance of receiving and sharing God's love in your life? Without God's Love we have

_____

we gain_____1 Corinthians 13:1-3

#-3. What must we do to receive Christ, the Heavenly Father, and His Spirit of Love within us?

_____

_____. John 14:21-23.

#–4. As disciples of Jesus we receive God's gift of love through the Holy Spirit because Jesus our Lord

_____ for us. John 17:26

#-5. When does the Father's Love that Jesus prayed for His disciples, enters into His disciples hearts?

_____

_____

_____Acts 2:38

#-6. What is the new commandment Jesus gave us to follow?

_____

_____John 13:34 & 35

What is the mark of a true disciple?

_____

_____

Will you learn and apply our Lord's new command?

_____

#–7. How does Jesus' new command raise our standard of love for one another over the 2nd command

_____

_____

John 13:34&35—Mark 12:31

#–8. How can we love one another as Jesus loved us? By putting on

_____

daily. Then making the expression of His

_____

a priority in our lives, then use the

_____

system during the day to make sure we are reflecting Jesus Spirit of love to others. Page 126.

#–9. What can we check for to see if we are expressing God's Love to others? Are we showing

_____,

and expressing _____,

to one another. 1 Corinthians 13:4

#–10. What are the outward expressions and virtues of God's indwelling Spirit of Love?

_____

_____

_____1 Corinthians 13:4-7

#–11. Are you receiving these expressions of God's love in the Church?

_____

Are you expressing the virtues of God's Love?

_____

#–12. What is our designed purpose in life?

_____

_____Romans 8:29

What must you do to fulfill your created purpose in life?

_____

_____

_____

Acts 2:37-38   John 14:21-23   1John 4:7-21.

"As the Father has loved Me, so have I loved you. Now remain in My Love, just as I have obeyed My Fathers commands and remain in His Love. I have told you this so that My joy may be in you and that your joy may be complete. My command is this: love each other as I have loved you." (John 15:9-12)

"Dear friends, since God so loved us, we also ought to love one another. None has ever seen God; but if we love one another, God lives in us and His Love is made complete in us." (1John 4:11-12)

"And so we know and rely on the love God has for us. God is love. Whoever lives in love lives in God, and God in him." (1John 4:16)

Reference Page

Reference:

Order and Complexity page   Reference "The Genesis Record" page 18 author Henry M. Morris.

"Outwitted" by Edwin Markham

"Barney the Butterfly" reference–"Parables Inc." January 1985.

Fireman story– unknown

Printed in the United States
73990LV00004B/175-207